Bible Study & Character-Building
Lesson Plans for
Families & Christian Educators
of Elementary-Aged Children

Christian Living

Helping YOU Share Christian Concepts with Kids

Christian Living

Published by Christian Concepts for Kids, Inc.

Copyright © 2024

All rights reserved.

Permission is granted to reproduce for ministry and family purposes only - not for resale.

Credits

Author/Publisher
Karen Palmer

Editors
Fresh Eyes Proofreaders
Grace Roderick
Judy Maples
Lee Burris
Susan Shami

Photographers
Addison Roderick
Karen Palmer

Artists
Addison Roderick
Grace Roderick
Julie Anna
Lee Burris
TJ Roderick

Outdoor Activity Contributor
Jeff Duke
Randy Gobel

Thank you! This book would not be possible without you.

Christian Living

Thirty one ways to help mentors engage with children about Christian Living through lessons, discussion topics, indoor and outdoor activites, and more.

Christian Concepts for Kids helps YOU share Christian concepts with elementary-aged kids. The discussions and activities provide amazing curriculum for homeschool, children's church, Sunday school, backyard Bible studies, summer camps, VBS, and other programs.

Our curriculum also provides parents and grandparents ideas for planning Christ-centered Family Fun Days and Grand Days (grandparents and grandchildren).

The discussions in this book cover sin, becoming a Christian, spiritual armor, praise, prayer, the Holy Spirit's fruit, His gifts, and His help for Christians.

For weekly programs: This book works well from April through October.

Table of Contents

Chapter 1 - Christian Living

Becoming a Christian	Page - 3
What Sin? Who's a Sinner?!?!	Page - 5
Christian Living	Page - 7
The Gift of Righteousness	Page - 9

Chapter 2 - A Look Back, A Look Forward

Remember Me	Page - 13
Remembering Our Moms	Page - 15
Remembering Our Waiter and Waitress	Page - 17
Remembering Our Leaders	Page - 19
Remembering Our Heroes	Page - 21

Chapter 3 - True Trust

Trashing Trust	Page - 25
Feelings and Trust	Page - 27
Pure Trust	Page - 29
Trusting Praise	Page - 31

Chapter 4 - Spiritual Armor

What is Spiritual Armor?	Page - 35
Truth and Righteousness	Page - 37
Peace and Faith	Page - 39
Salvation and the Word	Page - 41
Prayer	Page - 43

Chapter 5 - Praise

What is Praise?	Page - 47
Why Praise God?	Page - 49
Fellowship and Praise	Page - 51
Praising God	Page - 53

Chapter 6 - Forgiven

What is Forgiveness?	Page - 57
Why is Forgiveness Important?	Page - 59
Forgiving Others	Page - 61
Forgiven	Page - 63

Chapter 7 - Spiritual Gifts

What are Spiritual Gifts?	Page - 67
The Gifts	Page - 69
I Have Gifts!	Page - 71
Using My Gifts	Page - 73
Gifts and Love	Page - 75

Additional Information

Coming Soon	Page - 77
Supplemental Material	Page - 77
About Karen Palmer	Page - 77
Spiritual Armor Sample	Page - 78
Soldier Cutout	Page - 79
Armor Cutouts	Page - 80
Forgiven Fruit Solution	Page - 81

Chapter 1
Christian Living

Prayer Box

Becoming a Christian

Discussion: Becoming a Christian: Just how do we do that?
Craft: "Becoming a Christian" Game
Indoor Activity: "Becoming a Christian" Hunt
Outdoor Activity: "Becoming a Christian" Hunt

What Sin? Who's a Sinner?!?!

Discussion: This discussion answers these questions and leads children to know that we all have sinned and need a Savior.
Craft: I Am . . . Frame
Indoor Activity: Ten Commandments Race
Outdoor Activity: GOOD SHEPHERD Hunt

Christian Living

Discussion: This discussion focuses on the fruit that is produced as we live out our lives for Christ.
Craft: Prayer Box
Indoor Activity: Which Fruit? Theater
Outdoor Activity: What Do You See?

The Gift of Righteousness

Discussion: As we live out our lives as Christians, we receive help from the Holy Spirit to be a blessing to others and live toward the righteousness we receive from Jesus.
Craft: Pencil Case Prayers
Indoor Activity: Forgiven Frame
Outdoor Activity: "Thank You" Tree

Chapter 1: Christian Living

Devotional Doodles

Draw a Picture

Draw a picture of what Christian living means to you.

List Ten

List the Ten Commandments
Exodus 20:3-17

1. _____
2. _____
3. _____
4. _____
5. _____
6. _____
7. _____
8. _____
9. _____
10. _____

Find the Words

V	K	P	W	J	G	O	D	M	J
S	L	K	T	E	F	S	D	S	F
H	O	L	Y	S	P	I	R	I	T
T	V	T	H	U	O	N	T	N	H
J	E	J	L	S	U	E	H	N	J
U	V	K	S	R	L	J	N	E	I
T	M	G	B	B	E	U	M	R	K
C	H	R	I	S	T	I	A	N	M
M	N	B	F	O	R	G	I	V	E
Z	S	Q	M	D	F	N	I	C	R

SIN   SINNER   BIBLE
LOVE   CHRISTIAN   GOD
JESUS   FORGIVE   HOLY SPIRIT

Becoming a Christian

Prior to Discussion
- Have a Bible available and ask for volunteers to read.

Discussion

Ask: *Allow time for answers.*
- What does it mean to be a Christian?

Say:
- The word Christian refers to people who believe in Jesus.

Ask: *Allow time for discussion.*
- What do you think this means?
- What is the first step toward living a Christian life or becoming a Christian?

Say:
- We first need to know about sin.

Ask: *Allow time for answers.*
- What can you tell me about sin?
- What do Adam and Eve have to do with sin?

Say:
- Sin came into the world when Adam and Eve disobeyed God in the Garden of Eden.
- Even though God told them not to, Adam and Eve ate from the tree of the knowledge of good and evil.
- They brought sin into the life of mankind, and the punishment for sin is death.
- We are all born with this sin problem.

Ask: *Allow time for answers.*
- Knowing that each of us has this sin problem, what can we do about it?

Say:
- The Bible helps us see that God loves us enough to help us with this sin problem because He wants a relationship with each of us.
- He told His Old Testament prophets to write about a person who would come and take away the sins of the world.
- In the New Testament, we meet that person.

Ask: *Allow time for answers.*
- Who is this person?

Say:
- John the Baptist answers this question.

Read: John 1:29

Ask: *Allow time for answers.*
- What does this verse mean for you and me?

Say:
- The following verse gives us the Gospel, the good news of Christ!

Read: John 3:16

Say:
- When we believe in Jesus and accept His gift of forgiveness, our sins are not counted against us any longer.
- You and I, like Paul, can confess, "Jesus is my Lord!"

Read: Romans 10:9

Say:
- Forgiveness, salvation, and the promise of eternal life are the beginning of Christian living.
- Christian living is a relationship with Jesus.
- Spending time in prayer and reading God's words in the Bible help us really get to know our Lord.
- Waking in the morning and telling Him, "Good morning," and "I love you," is a great way to begin our day.
- As our relationship grows, our faith and trust in Him grows.
- As our faith and trust build, we truly believe that He always knows what is best for us.
- We will want Him to lead our life.

Final Thought:

Being a Christian and allowing Jesus to be our Lord can be difficult at times. Knowing that we are forgiven and saved from our sins is awesome. Knowing that we have eternal life is the best feeling ever. Asking Jesus to be our Lord is the first step in a very special relationship. Living a life of obedience is a way to tell Him, "Thank you." and that we love Him.

Becoming a Christian — Activities

Craft: "Becoming a Christian" Game

Items Needed:
- General: Markers or Crayons
- Per Child: 6 Craft Sticks and an Apron

Instructions:
- Tell the children that they will be making a "Becoming a Christian" game.
- Give each child six craft sticks.
- Using the markers or crayons, the children will write a verse, draw an image, or print words on one side of each craft stick that pertains to becoming a Christian.
- The child's name will be written on the other side.
- Tell the children that they can play the "Becoming a Christian" game with their family and friends.
- They will play the game by hiding the sticks so others can search for them.
- They may even ask about the meaning of the verse, image, or words.
- This gives you the opportunity to tell them more!

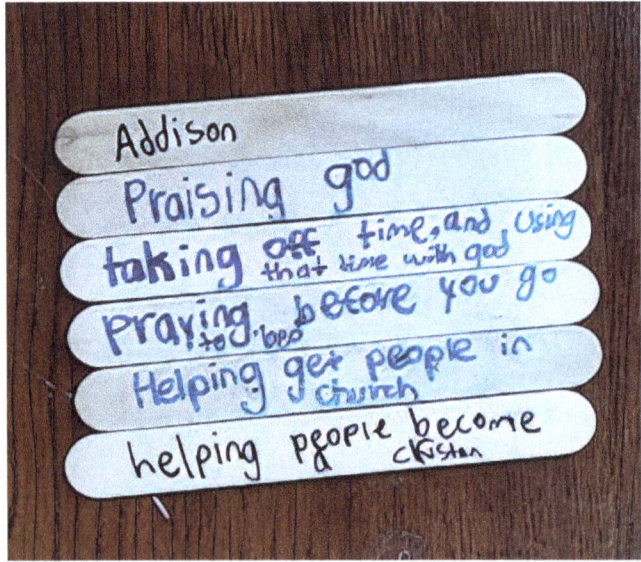

Indoor Activity: "Becoming a Christian" Hunt

Prior to Activity:
- Hide the sticks around the room.

Items Needed:
- Sticks from craft: ("Becoming a Christian" Game) or 20 Craft Sticks with verses, images, or words about becoming a Christian on each one (Bible, Cross, Jesus, Praying Hands, Prayer, Forgiven, Empty Grave, Holy Spirit, etc.)

Instructions:
- Tell the children that there are twenty "Becoming a Christian" sticks hidden around the room.
- Have the children look around the room to find the hidden sticks.
- The child who finds the most sticks wins the game.
- Have each child hold up his or her sticks and discuss what is on each stick.

Outdoor Activity: "Becoming a Christian" Hunt

Prior to Activity:
- Hide the sticks around outside.

Items Needed:
- Sticks from craft: ("Becoming a Christian Game") or 20 Craft Sticks with verses, images, or words about becoming a Christian on each one (Bible, Cross, Jesus, Praying Hands, Prayer, Forgiven, Empty Grave, Holy Spirit, etc.)

Instructions:
- Tell the children that there are twenty "Becoming a Christian" sticks hidden outside.
- Have the children search and find the hidden sticks.
- The child who finds the most sticks wins the game.
- Have each child hold up his or her sticks and discuss what is on each stick.

What Sin? Who's a Sinner?!?!

Prior to Discussion
- Have a Bible available and ask for volunteers to read.

Discussion
Ask: *Allow time for answers.*
- Have you ever heard, "Knowing is half the battle?"

Say:
- This means that you have to know about something before it means something.
- Knowing gives us opportunities.

Ask: *Allow time for answers.*
- Would you love your favorite food if you never tasted it?
- Does knowing how to read or calculate numbers help you?
- What are some other important things to know?
- Do you think sin could be on our list?
- What is sin?

Say:
- Sin is doing things that are wrong or not doing the right things.

Ask: *Allow time for answers.*
- What can you tell me about Adam and Eve's connection to sin?

Say:
- Adam and Eve lived in the Garden of Eden and they didn't know what sin was, but that changed.

Read: Genesis 2:15-17
Read: Genesis 3:6-7
Read: Genesis 3:22

Ask: *Allow time for answers.*
- What does this story have to do with us?

Say:
- This is when sin entered the world.
- And this affects everyone!

Read: John 3:23
Ask: *Allow time for answers.*
- Do you know the punishment for sin?

Say:
- Paul tells us that the punishment (wages) is death.

Read: Romans 6:23
Ask: *Allow time for answers.*
- What can we do about our sin? *Confess our sin.*
- So what does it mean to confess our sin?

Say:
- When we confess our sins, we admit that we have sinned, we are sorry, and we repent or turn away from the sin.

Ask: *Allow time for answers.*
- What happens when we confess our sins?

Read: 1 John 1:9
Say:
- God has provided a way for us to be forgiven of our sins and saved from the punishment.
- We, then, become righteous and gain eternal life.

Read: John 3:16
Say:
- God has given us this gift because He loves us so much!

Final Thought:
Even though everyone has sinned, God still loves us anyway. Because of that love, He sent His Son, Jesus, to take our punishment. Jesus died and took our sins to the cross with Him. By confessing our sins and accepting Jesus' gift of forgiveness, we become righteous and our sins are not counted against us anymore. If you want to talk more about accepting Jesus' gift of forgiveness and eternal life, let me know and we can talk more about it.

Chapter 1: Christian Living

What Sin? Who's a Sinner?!?! — Activities

Craft: I Am . . . Frame

Items Needed:
- General: String or Yarn, Glue, and Markers or Colored Pencils
- Per Child: 1 Bible, 1 Sheet of Construction Paper, and Craft Sticks (enough to create a frame around the construction paper)

Instructions:
- Give the children the supplies.
- Tell the children to find 1 Corinthians 13:4.
- The children will write 1 Corinthians 13:4-6 on the construction paper, but will replace the words "love" or "it" with their own names.
- Each child will use the sticks to create a frame for the construction paper and the string to create a way to hang the artwork.
- While they are working, open a discussion about Jesus' commands to love God first and most and to love others as we love ourselves, asking if obeying Jesus' commands is always easy.

Indoor Activity: Ten Commandments Race

Prior to Activity: (*for saving time or for younger children*)
- Write the Ten Commandments on the cards.
- The Ten Commandments can be found in Exodus 20:3-17.

Items Needed:
- 2 Bibles and 20 Large Index Cards

Instructions:
- Divide the children into two teams.
- Give each team ten cards and a Bible.
- They will find the Ten Commandments in Exodus 20:3-17.
- Have each team write one of the Ten Commandments on each card and mix the cards up.
- The teams will swap cards.
- Each team will put the Ten Commandments cards in order according to Exodus 20:3-17.
- The first team to have the Commandments in the correct order wins the game.

Outdoor Activity: GOOD SHEPHERD Hunt

Items Needed:
- Per Team: 1 Paper Lunch Bag

Instructions:
- Divide the children into groups of 2 or 3.
- Give each team a paper bag.
- Have each team find things outside that start with each letter of: GOOD SHEPHERD.
- The group that gets all of their items first wins.
- This game can be played again with different words: FORGIVENESS, SHEEP, HOLY SPIRIT, or JESUS.

Variation:
- The game can be timed, and the team with the most items wins the game.

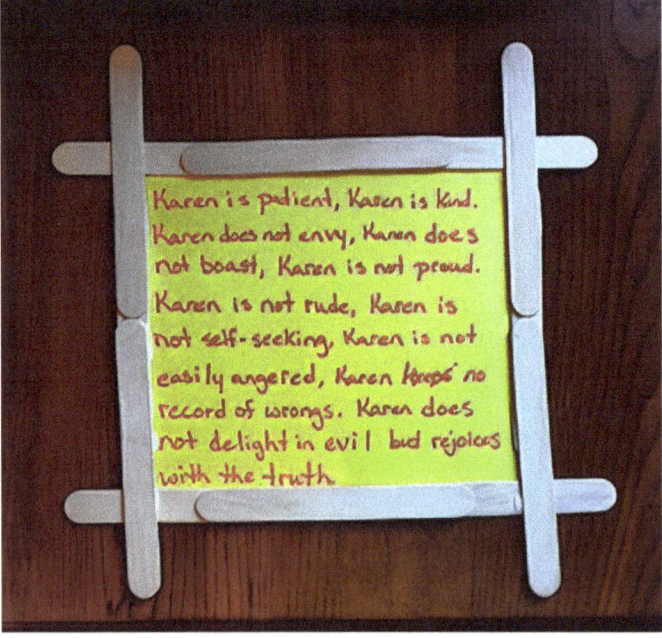

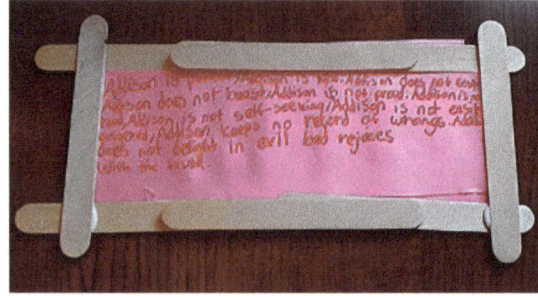

Christian Living

Prior to Discussion
- Have a Bible available and ask for volunteers to read.

Discussion
Say:
- Jesus warns us about wolves in sheep's clothing.

Read: Matthew 7:15

Ask: *Allow time for answers.*
- What does this mean?

Say:
- Jesus is talking about people who pretend to be good.

Ask: *Allow time for answers.*
- What does it mean to pretend to be good?
- So, if there are people who look like they are good, but they are not, what did Jesus say to watch for to determine the difference?

Read: Matthew 7:15-18

Ask: *Allow time for answers.*
- What fruit is Jesus talking about?

Say:
- The fruit of the Spirit!

Ask: *Allow time for answers.*
- Can you name the fruit of the Spirit?

Read: Galatians 5:22-23

Ask: *Allow time for answers.*
- Can someone's fruit tell you a lot about that person?

Say:
- Jesus is telling us that we need to pay attention to people's actions and attitudes to watch the fruit.

Ask: *Allow time for answers.*
- Whose fruit do we need to pay the most attention to?

Say:
- We need to pay the closest attention to our own fruit.
- We can take care of the fruit in our lives just as we would take care of a fruit tree.
- Bad fruit needs to be picked off fruit trees so the good fruit can receive more nutrients.
- The tree can't send any resources to rotten fruit if it has been removed.
- We need to check our lives for bad fruit, the opposite of the Spirit's fruit, and get rid of it.
- When our sinful fruit is removed from our life, the good fruit will receive more of our time, finances, attention, etc.
- A healthy tree needs fresh air, sunshine, water, and good soil to produce great fruit.
- We need to love God, other people, and allow the Holy Spirit to give us His fruit.

Read: Mark 12:30-31

Say:
- When we obey these commands, we produce fruit of the Spirit.
- Doing things in a Spirit-fruit way is always the best way.

Final Thought:
We can look at other people and see the fruit that they produce, and we learn a lot about those people. The most important person that we need to watch for the fruit is ourselves. When we see bad fruit in our own life, we can get rid of it. We can become better at producing Spirit fruit when we act in a Spirit-fruit way, loving God and others as Jesus commanded.

Christian Living — Activities

Craft: Prayer Box

Items Needed:
- General: 1/4 to 1/2 Yard of Fabric, Bias Tape (strips of fabric for corners: fabric store will have this - choose some to match the fabric), Measuring Stick or Tape, Glue, Scissors, and Ribbon (optional)
- Per Child: 1 Empty Cube-Shaped Tissue Box

Instructions:
- Using the supplies, each child will measure the tissue box and measure and cut pieces of the fabric to cover each side of the tissue box.
- The bias tape will be glued over the fabric where the edges meet.
- The boxes will be placed in an area where everyone can see them.
- The children will create "note paper" by cutting the construction paper into different shapes and sizes, making sure that the "note paper" is large enough to write a note.
- The "note paper" will be placed in front of the boxes for prayers to be written on and placed in the box.
- They will write at least one prayer for each family member and place it in the box.
- Each day the family can gather and pray for everything in the box.

Variation:
- Construction paper may be used in place of the fabric and bias tape.

Indoor Activity: Which Fruit? Theater

Items Needed:
- General: 1 Bible, 9 Pieces of Yellow Paper, Two Bags, and Pencils or Pens
- Per Child: 1/2 Sheet of White Paper

Instructions:
- Divide the children into teams of two.
- Write one fruit of the Spirit on each piece of yellow paper and place the paper in a bag. (See Galatians 5:22-23).
- Each child will write a difficult situation on the white paper and place it in the other bag.
- Examples: Failing Grades, A Sick Loved One, Parent Loses their Job, Dropped Your Lunch in the Dirt, Your Best Friend Moves Far Away, Your Friend is Being Bullied, Your Grandparent is Involved in a Car Wreck
- One team will draw a piece of paper from each bag.
- One team member will read the situation, but not mention the fruit that was chosen.
- He or she will act out a response to the situation that is the opposite of the Spirit fruit that was chosen.
- The second team member will act out a response that **IS** the Spirit fruit that the team chose.
- Other teams will guess which fruit was chosen.
- The team that guesses correctly goes next.

Outdoor Activity: What Do You See?

Items Needed:
- Per Team: 1 Magnifying Glass, 1 Pad of Paper, and 1 Pencil or Pen

Instructions:
- Divide the children into teams of two or three (teams do not need to be even).
- Give each team a magnifying glass.
- Explain that each team will look at things in the outdoors through the magnifying glass.
- Each team will write what they are looking at (for example, a leaf) and what they see looking through the magnifying glass that they did not see without it.
- Bring the teams together and give each team some time to talk about what they wrote on their paper.
- Open a discussion asking how the Bible can act as a magnifying glass in our life.

The Gift of Righteousness

Prior to Discussion
- Have a Bible available and ask for volunteers to read.

Discussion
Say:
- Sin came into the world with Adam and Eve.

Ask: *Allow time for answers.*
- What can you tell me about Adam and Eve?

Say:
- Adam and Eve disobeyed God when they ate from the tree of the knowledge of good and evil.
- This brought sin into the life of mankind.

Ask: *Allow time for answers.*
- Who is affected by this sin? *Everyone.*

Say:
- Now every human being is born with this sinful nature and needs help to become righteous.

Ask: *Allow time for answers.*
- How can we become righteous?

Read: Romans 3:22
Say:
- We receive righteousness through faith in Jesus.
- Faith, or truly believing in Jesus is the very beginning of a Christian life.
- Believing is the first step of faith that every Christian makes.
- Then, we confess with our mouth that our Lord is Jesus.

Read: Romans 10:9
Ask: *Allow time for answers.*
- After we are saved from sin through Jesus and become a Christian, what's next?

. **Say:**
- We need to pay attention to our fruit.
- When we see that we are producing the opposite of spiritual fruit we know that we need help.
- We are like a fruit tree that needs an arborist: someone who cares for trees.

Ask: *Allow time for answers.*
- Who can help us produce better fruit? *the Holy Spirit*

Say:
- Jesus knew that we need help, so He prayed to God to send the Holy Spirit.

Read: John 14:16-17
Say:
- The Holy Spirit is our advocate, counselor, helper and comforter.
- He lives with us to help guide us.

Read: John 16:13
Say:
- The Holy Spirit helps us discover and develop our spiritual gifts and fulfill our special purpose: the reason God created each of us.
- As we read the Bible, pray, and listen to the Holy Spirit, we grow closer to God and it helps us be obedient.

Ask: *Allow time for answers.*
- What are the two most important commands that Jesus gave us?

Read: Mark 12:29-31
Ask: *Allow time for answers.*
- When we love God first and most, and love other people as we love ourselves, are we obeying our Lord and producing Spiritual fruit?

Final Thought:
We have the best King, Lord, and Savior ever! He loves us more than we are able to understand. We are called to be a Kingdom family who has a King that offers the gift of righteousness. He graciously bestows blessings on us as we obey Him and produce Spirit fruit. Obeying our Lord is also a great way to show Him that we love Him.

Chapter 1: Christian Living

The Gift of Righteousness — Activities

Craft: Pencil Case Prayers
Items Needed:
- General: 1 Bible, Markers or Crayons, Scissors, Glue
- Per Child: 1/2 Sheet of Construction Paper and Scrap Construction Paper

Instructions:
- Give each child the supplies.
- Tell the children to fold the paper over 1/3 and then again 1/3 and glue in place.
- They will use the scrap construction paper to glue a piece to cover and enclose the bottom of the pencil case.
- Using the markers or crayons, each child will decorate the case.
- When the cases are complete, the pencils will be placed inside the cases.
- Place all of the cases together and ask each child to pray for the people who touch the case or pencils.
- Pray that the Holy Spirit will help each person who touches the pencils or pencil cases in a way that is special to him or her.
- While they are working, read Acts 19:11-12 and open a discussion about their thoughts.

Indoor Activity: Forgiven Frame
Items Needed:
- General: Craft Sticks, String or Yarn, Glue, and Markers or Colored Pencils
- Per Child: 1 Plastic Mirror, 1 Photo, or 1/4 Sheet of Drawing Paper

Instructions:
- Give the children the supplies.
- If you are using the drawing paper, they will draw their portrait on the paper.
- The sticks will be used to create a frame around the mirror, photo, or portrait.
- The string or yarn will be used to create a hanger.
- They will write "SINNER" on the top stick on the frame.
- They will then glue one stick over the "SINNER" stick and write "FORGIVEN" on the new top stick.
- While they are working, open a discussion asking how sinners can be forgiven. Lead them to the fact that we are forgiven when we accept the forgiveness offered through Jesus.

Outdoor Activity: "Thank You" Tree
Items Needed:
- General: Paint, Paint Brushes, A Few Cups of Water (to rinse brushes), Tree, Shovel, and Garden Gloves
- Per Child: 1 Fist-Sized Rock, Apron, and Garden Gloves

Instructions:
- Plant the tree or choose one that is already planted.
- Each child will paint a rock in a way that conveys being thankful for the person or people who told the child about Jesus.
- When the rocks dry, the children will place the rocks around the "thank you" tree.
- Their rocks and the tree will stand as a thank you to everyone who shares Jesus with someone else.

Chapter 2
A Look Back, A Look Forward

Leah, TJ, Grace, Addison making reminder rocks

Remember Me
Discussion: What fruit are you bearing? When you leave a room, what fruit are you leaving behind for people to remember about you?
Craft: Remember Me
Indoor Activity: What's in the Bag?
Outdoor Activity: Remember This

Remembering Our Moms
Discussion: A special day and a special discussion for mothers. How can we show appreciation for all they do?
Craft: Mom's Coupon Book
Indoor Activity: To Do List
Outdoor Activity: Flower Bouquet

Remembering Our Waiter and Waitress
Discussion: Many verses in the Bible tell us to serve others. How do we honor and appreciate those who serve us?
Craft: Reminder Rocks
Indoor Activity: Eating Out
Outdoor Activity: Serving Others

Remembering Our Leaders
Discussion: In an election year, we hear a lot of differing political opinions. This discussion looks at what the Bible says about leaders.
Craft: Letters to Leaders
Indoor Activity: Lead My Story
Outdoor Activity: Follow the Leader

Remembering Our Heroes
Discussion: This discussion helps children think about what makes a person a hero and appreciate the real ones in our lives.
Craft: Appreciation for Heroes
Indoor Activity: Helping Our Heroes
Outdoor Activity: Help the Heroes Relay

Chapter 2: A Look Back, A Look Forward

Devotional Doodles
Draw a Picture

Draw a picture of how you want to be remembered.

10 Words

Write ten words that describe how you want to be remembered.

1. _____
2. _____
3. _____
4. _____
5. _____
6. _____
7. _____
8. _____
9. _____
10. _____

Find the Words

V	K	H	W	J	G	M	M	E
S	L	E	A	D	E	R	S	O	F
H	W	R	Y	S	P	I	R	I	M
T	A	O	H	U	R	N	T	N	H
J	I	E	L	S	A	E	H	N	W
U	T	S	S	R	Y	J	N	B	A
T	R	G	B	B	E	U	M	I	I
C	E	R	I	S	R	I	A	B	T
M	S	B	F	O	R	G	I	L	E
Z	S	R	E	M	E	M	B	E	R

REMEMBER   MOM   ME
WAITER   LEADERS   BIBLE
WAITRESS   HEROES   PRAYER

Christian Living

Remember Me

Prior to Discussion
- Have a Bible available and ask for volunteers to read.
- For each child, have one index card.
- Write the fruit of the Spirit listed in Galatians 5:22-23 on a chalkboard, white board, or poster board to refer to during the discussion.

Discussion
Say:
- The fruit of the Spirit is a list of positive characteristics the Holy Spirit gives us.
- They are called fruit because we bear them, just as a fruit tree bears its fruit.
- A person's fruit says a lot about them, just as a tree says a lot about it by the fruit it bears.
- The fruit of the Spirit we bear helps people describe us and remember us.

Read: Galatians 5:22-23

Say: *Pointing to the list.*
- The fruit of the Spirit is written down so we can refer to it during the discussion.
- Let's talk about some people and discuss memories and the fruit each one bears.

Ask: *Allow time for discussion.*
- Tell me some words you think of when I mention these names:
  » Jesus
  » Your Mom or Dad
  » Your Grandma or Grandpa
  » Jesus' Mother, Mary
  » Noah (from the Bible - he built the ark)
  » Your Friend
  » Your Teacher

Say:
- Everyone has memories of other people.
- When those people are not around, the memories help us remember them.

Ask: *Allow time for answers.*
- What memories do you think people have about you?
- Do you think they are nice memories?
- What words do you think they would use to describe you?

Say:
- Let's do a little activity.
- Close your eyes and imagine you are going out of town to spend one week visiting family.
- Think about some of the things you would like to do with your family. *Allow time for thoughts.*
- Think about the food you would eat and the conversation you would have while sitting at the dinner table. *Allow time for thoughts.*
- Imagine yourself playing with family members your own age. *Allow time for thoughts.*
- Now imagine the week is over, and it would be time to go back home.
- Imagine how you feel about leaving.
- Imagine how your family feels about you leaving.
- You can open your eyes now.

Ask: *Allow time for answers.*
- What do you think your family would say about your time together?
- What fruit of the Spirit would they remember about you?

Say: *Pointing to the list.*
- When we are around other people, we are making memories and showing them our fruit.
- Let's do another activity.
- We will write fruit-words or reminder-words that describe each other.

Action:
- Give each child an index card and ask them to write their name at the top.
- They are to pass the card to the person on their right.
- When the children receive the cards, they will each write words that describe the child whose name is on the card and pass it to the person on their right.
- This will continue until the cards get back to the child whose name is on the card.
- Have each child read the words that are written on his or her card and decide which one he or she likes best.

Say:
- We can control what people remember about us by changing our attitudes and the way we treat other people.

Read: John 13:34-35

Final Thought:
When we are around other people, we can treat them the way Jesus wants us to. We leave others with reminders. Let's think about the fruit we bear and the memories we leave behind. Will Jesus be happy about the reminders we leave? Will they see the fruit of the Spirit?

Remember Me — Activities

Chapter 2: A Look Back, A Look Forward

Craft: Remember Me

Items Needed:
- General: Crayons or Markers
- Per Child: 1 Sheet of White Copy Paper

Instructions:
- Give each child one sheet of white paper.
- Have them each put their name on the top of the paper and draw their portrait on the paper, leaving about 2 inches of room at the bottom of the paper.
- After they have finished their portraits, have them each write the words on their index cards (from the discussion) on the bottom of their portrait.
- While they are working, discuss different memory words they would like people to use when thinking about them.

Variation:
- Have the children pass their portraits around the room for other children to write memory words for each other on the bottom of the portraits.
- Have the children glue the index cards from the discussion to the paper.

Indoor Activity: What's in the Bag

Prior to Activity:
- Place small items (see list below) in the bag so the children don't know what is in the bag.

Items Needed:
- 1 Sheet of Paper for Each Child, 1 Pencil or Pen for Each Child, 1 Bag (that you can't see through), and Different Items to Put in the Bag (cookie cutters, small toys, lollypops, spools of thread, etc.)

Instructions:
- Have each child take a turn reaching his or her hand into the bag to feel the items, while everyone counts slowly to 10 or 15.
- They cannot look in the bag.
- When his or her time is up, he or she will write down what he or she thinks is in the bag.

Variation:
- If there are younger children, you can allow them to draw pictures.
- You can partner a younger child with an older child who can write down the words. They can both reach their hands in the bag.

Outdoor Activity: Remember This

Instructions:
- Have the children stand in a circle.
- Choose one child to start the game.
- The child who starts the game will do something such as pat his or her head, twirl around in a circle, jump up and down, etc.
- The child next to him or her will repeat the action and do something else.
- The next child will repeat the first two actions and do something else.
- This will continue around the circle.
- If a child can't do all of the actions, he or she is out of the game.
- The last child to do all of the actions wins the game.

Remembering Our Moms

Prior to Discussion
- Have a Bible available and ask for volunteers to read.

Discussion
Ask:
- Who knows what today is?

Say:
- It is Mother's Day!

Ask: *Allow time for answers.*
- Why do we even have Mother's Day?

Say:
- It is the day that we show appreciation to our moms for all that they do for us.

Ask: *Allow time for answers.*
- Can any of you think of some things that your mom has done for you this past year?

Say:
- Our moms help us in so very many ways.

Ask: *Allow time for answers.*
- When your mom does these things for you, do you let her know that you appreciate and love her?
- What are some ways we can show mom that we love and appreciate her and all that she does for us?

Say:
- The Bible tells us some things that we can do.

Read: Exodus 20:12
Ask: *Allow time for answers.*
- What does it mean to honor our mother and father?

Say:
- Honor means to show a courteous regard for someone.
- This means we are polite, well-mannered, and considerate to someone.

Read: Leviticus 19:3
Ask: *Allow time for answers.*
- What does it mean to respect your mother and father?

Say:
- Respect means to show consideration or regard for someone.
- This means that we are thoughtful, kind, concerned, and show respect to someone.
- Here is something else that the Bible tells us that we can do for our moms.

Read: Proverbs 6:20
Ask: *Allow time for answers.*
- What do you think this verse means?

Say:
- This means that we should listen to our dad and mom when they give us rules or teach us things.

Ask: *Allow time for answers.*
- How can we show our moms that we are listening to what they teach us?

Say:
- Since our moms help us in so many ways, let's think of things that we can do to show our appreciation, respect, consideration, and kindness to our moms. *Allow time for responses.*

Final Thought:

For mom's special day, let's try to do the things that the Bible tells us to do for our moms. Let's go home and show our moms that we love, care for, and appreciate them. It will make your mom and God happy.

Remembering Our Moms

Craft: Mom's Coupon Book

Prior to Craft: (*optional*)
- Doing the indoor activity gives the children ideas for the booklets.

Items Needed:
- General: Scissors and Crayons or Markers
- Per Child: 1/2 Sheet of Construction Paper and 2 Sheets of White Copy Paper

Instructions:
- Have the children cut the 1/2 sheet of construction paper in half. This will be the front and back covers for their books.
- Have the children cut the two pieces of white paper in half and then cut those in half so they have 4 pieces from each sheet of white paper, 8 total.
- They are to put the sheets together with the construction paper on the outside and staple on one edge to create a booklet.
- On the outside of the booklet, ask them to write "Mom's Coupon Book."
- Inside of their booklets, they are to create coupons for things that they will do for their moms when asked.
- Mom can tear out the coupon and redeem it when she wants that particular thing done.

Indoor Activity: To Do List

Items Needed:
- Poster Board, or White Board and Erasable Markers, or Chalk Board and Chalk

Instructions:
- The children will take turns writing things on the board that they can do for mom to make her feel special, know that she is loved and appreciated, and help her in some way.
- Examples of things that they could do are:
  » Cleaning their room.
  » Giving mom flowers.
  » Helping cook dinner.
  » Setting the table for dinner.
  » Cleaning up after dinner.
  » Helping a younger sibling with homework or a chore.
  » Reminding mom that we love her by telling her, "I love you."
  » Giving mom a kiss and hug.
- Leave the list on the board for the craft.

Outdoor Activity: Flower Bouquet

Submitted by: Randy Gobel

- If there are flowers that the children can pick that people don't mind them picking and are not poisonous, allow the children to go outside to pick flowers for their moms.
- The children can give the flowers to their mom or grandmother.

Chapter 2: A Look Back, A Look Forward

Remembering Our Waiter and Waitress

Prior to Discussion
- Have a Bible available and ask for volunteers to read.

Discussion
Ask:
- Did you know that Jesus said that we need to serve others if we want to be great?

Read: Mark 10:42-45

Say:
- When we are doing things for other people, we are showing kindness just like Jesus did.
- When we make time for other people, we are showing them that they are important to us.
- When we take our time to provide for the needs of others, we are great in God's eyes!

Ask:
- Would you rather be sitting at a table in a restaurant, or being a waiter or waitress in one?
- Did you know that Jesus talks about this?

Read: Luke 22:26-27

Say:
- Jesus is saying that if we want to be great LIKE HIM, we need to serve like HIM.
- We don't need to try to be great in the world's eyes.
- We need to try to be great in God's eyes.

Ask: *Allow time for answers.*
- What are some other servant jobs that people have that help others, or serve others? *Examples are: policeman, fireman, doctor, nurse, minister, teacher, waiter, waitress, mailman, cashier at store, hair stylist, etc.*

Say:
- Serving other people is a tough thing to do because you give a lot of yourself when you serve others.
- We need to try to remember to let them know we appreciate their service.

Ask: *Allow time for answers.*
- What are some ways we could show our appreciation to people that serve us?
- Do you think saying, "Thank you." would be good?
- Do you think they would appreciate hearing that they are doing a good job?
- What if you told them that you were going to pray for them at bedtime tonight?

Say:
- We all like to be appreciated.
- It is nice to let other people know that we appreciate all of the things that they do to serve other people.

Final Thought:
What other people think is great is not the same thing that God thinks is great. When we see someone serving others in the restaurant, at the doctor's office, the hair salon, or the emergency vehicle driving down the road, remember that they are serving others. They are doing what Jesus wants us all to do. Let's remember to let them know that we appreciate them and their work.

Christian Living

Chapter 2: A Look Back, A Look Forward

Remembering Our Waiter and Waitress — Activities

Craft: Reminder Rocks

Submitted By: Jessica Roderick

Items Needed:
- General: Paint Brushes, Craft Supplies, and Craft Paint
- Per Child: 1 Small Rock

Instructions:
- Give each child one small rock, a paint brush, and some craft paint.
- Ask them to paint their rock with something that says, "Thank you," "Good job," "I appreciate you," or something else to let someone know that they are appreciated.
- They can paint the words on their rocks or draw an image such as a smiley face.
- Let them know that their rock is to be given to someone who serves them.
- When they give the rock away, they are to let that person know that the rock is a reminder for them that:
  » We appreciate them.
  » We will pray for them.
  » Werving other people makes us great in God's eyes.

Indoor Activity: Eating Out

Items Needed:
- General: Snacks, Drinks, Plates or Napkins, and Cups

Instructions:
- Ask for volunteers.
- Have the volunteers be the waiters and waitresses for the other children.
- These children will pass out the plates, cups, and food to the children who are sitting down.
- The teacher may need to serve the drink, depending on the children's ages.
- Remind the children who are sitting down being served to thank the waiters and waitresses and show appreciation for their work.
- When everyone has been served, ask the volunteers to sit down and the teacher can then serve them.

Outdoor Activity: Serving Others

Instructions:
- The children will act out different jobs in this activity.
- Let the children know that there are many jobs people have that allow them to serve other people.
- They are to think of some servant jobs to act out either individually or as a group.
- They are to think of a skit (a short funny play) to act out.
- They can use sticks, leaves, and other things from outside as props for their skits.
- If the children are gifted in this, you could ask your church leaders if they could act it out for the congregation during the service so they can serve others by doing their skit.

Addison's Reminder Rock

Chapter 2: A Look Back, A Look Forward

Remembering Our Leaders

Prior to Discussion
- Have a Bible available and ask for volunteers to read.

Discussion
Say:
- This discussion is about leaders and what we can do for them.

Ask: *Allow time for answers.*
- Who are some leaders in our country?
- Who are some leaders in our community?
- Do you think everyone agrees with our leaders?
- If we disagree with them, should we still care about them or want to help them? *Steer them to the answer being yes.*
- Why? *If anyone says that God put them in their positions, congratulate that child.*

Say:
- God has put all leaders in their positions!

Read: Romans 13:1
Say:
- If God put the leaders in their positions, we need to support God's choice by supporting our leaders.

Ask: *Allow time for answers.*
- How do you think we could support God's choice for our leaders?
- Do you think when we help them, we are supporting God's choice in our leaders?
- What could YOU possibly do to help our leaders?

Say:
- God tells us what we can all do for our leaders.

Read: 1 Timothy 2:1-3
Ask:
- Did you know that God said for us to pray for our leaders?
- Did you know that God wants us to give thanks for them?

Say:
- These are specific things that God wants us to do when it comes to our leaders.
- God didn't say that we should do these things if we feel like it or if we agree with them, but we should do them because God put them in their positions.
- Let's say a prayer for our leaders right now and thank God for them.

Action:
- Say a prayer for the leaders in your country and your local community.
- Allow the children to say prayers if they feel comfortable doing so.

Ask:
- Do you think it makes God happy when we do what He asks us to do?
- Do you think God is happy when we pray for our leaders, even when we don't agree with them?

Final Thought:
God loves for us to do what He asks us to do. He loves for us to accept and support His decisions and choices. When He puts people in leadership positions, we need to remember that He put them in their positions. We need to support His choice and help them in any ways we can. One huge way is to pray for them.

Chapter 2: A Look Back, A Look Forward

Remembering Our Leaders — Activities

Craft: Letters to Leaders
Items Needed:
General: Addresses for Leaders, White Paper, Pencils, Crayons or Markers, Stamps, and Envelopes

Instructions:
- Have the children write letters to their leaders. Younger children can draw pictures.
- Talk to the children about things that they can write to their leaders.
- They can write that:
  » They are praying for them.
  » They hope they have a great week.
  » God will guide them in their decisions.
  » They know they have a hard job and thank them for their hard work.
- When the letters are complete, the children can (if they are able) address the envelopes, put their return address, and put the stamp on it.
- Let the children know you will mail the letters.

Indoor Activity: Lead My Story
Instructions:
- Have the children sit in a circle.
- Designate one child as the "Story Starter" and have that child begin a story (one or two sentences only) about a leader (church leader, government leader, school leader, etc.).
- The child sitting next to the "Story Starter" will continue the story with one or two more sentences.
- The story will continue around the circle until everyone has added to the story twice.
- When that story is finished, choose another "Story Starter" to start another leadership story.

Outdoor Activity: Follow the Leader
- Choose one child as the "Leader" and have the other children pray for their new leader.
- Ask the children to line up single file behind the "Leader."
- The "Leader" will think of things to do (walking like a duck, running, jumping, walking, waving his hands in the air, praying, etc.) and all of the children are to do whatever the leader does as they follow him around.
- Allow the leader to do several things and then choose another child who has not had a chance to be the leader.
- Have the children pray for each new leader.

Chapter 2: A Look Back, A Look Forward

Remembering Our Heroes

Prior to Discussion
- Have a Bible available and ask for volunteers to read.

Discussion

Say:
- Our discussion today is about remembering our heroes.

Ask: *Allow time for answers.*
- What makes someone a hero?
- Is a hero someone who is really good at playing sports?
- Is a hero someone who pretends to be someone else on television or in the movies?
- Is a hero someone who gives someone his favorite cookie?

Say:
- Some people think these groups of people are heroes, and they can be.
- The heroes that we are talking about today are the people who risk and sometimes lose their lives to help someone else.
- The Bible tells us that there is no greater love than to lay down your life for someone else.

Read: John 15:13

Say:
- Memorial Day is a day that was set aside as a holiday to remember the men and women who died while serving in the American military.
- We are going to talk about the military heroes as well as other heroes in our lives.

Ask: *Allow time for answers.*
- Does anyone know someone who is a hero?
- What does that person do that lets you know that he or she is a hero?
- Can you think of some heroes in the Bible? *Examples: Moses, King David, Esther, Paul, John, and Jesus*
- What did they do that makes you think they are heroes?

Say:
- Some Bible heroes are:
  » Moses - He led God's people out of Egypt.
  » King David - Before he became King, David fought Goliath, the giant, to stop him from harming God's people; and then became King of Israel.
  » Daniel - He risked his life by praying to God, and his faith led the king to have faith in God.
  » Esther - She saved her people by going to the king.
  » Paul - He risked his life and went to prison for telling other people about Jesus and preaching the Gospel.
  » Jesus - Gave His life for us to be forgiven.

Ask:
- Can we let these people from the Bible times know that we appreciate them?
- Who are some heroes that we can show our appreciation to today? *Examples: Firemen, Policemen, Missionaries, Military, Emergency Workers*
- What could we do to let them know we are remembering and supporting them?

Say:
- These are all great suggestions!
- Since praying is always a great thing to do, let's say a prayer for them.

Action:
- Say a prayer for the heroes.
- Allow the children to pray if they feel comfortable doing so.

Final Thought:
When we think of heroes, we need to remember that they are risking their lives to help other people. We need to remember to pray for their safety and for God to help them while they are helping other people. We can also try to think of ways to let them know we are praying for them and that we appreciate them. Let's try to remember our heroes.

Christian Living

Chapter 2: A Look Back, A Look Forward

Remembering Our Heroes — Activities

Craft: Appreciation For Heroes

Items Needed:
- General: Scissors, Construction Paper, White Copy Paper, Crayons or Markers, and Decorations

Instructions:
- Ask the children to think of a group of heroes who they would like to help: a fire department, police department, military base nearby, missionaries, etc.
- Have the children make cards, pictures, and letters to send to their heroes.
- Let the children know you will take their cards, pictures, and letters to the heroes.
- They can thank their heroes and let them know they appreciate them, are praying for their safety, and for God to be with them as they do their work.

Indoor Activity: Helping Our Heroes

Items Needed:
- General: Cardboard Boxes, Poster Board, Markers or Crayons

Instructions:
- Let the children know they will be asking the church to bring in donations for our military heroes or their families.
- Allow the children to decide if they want to send their package to the men and women or to their children.
- Have the children decorate the box and poster board to let people know this is where they are to bring their donations.
- Ask two children to volunteer to speak to the church or other group to ask for donations to send to the military men and women or to children whose mother or father is deployed.
- Give the group one or two weeks to bring in their donations and send off the package.
- Part of the donations can be money to help with shipping.
- Any military base can give you an address for where to send your package.
- The children can write letters and draw pictures to put in the box as well.

Outdoor Activity: Help the Heroes Relay

Items Needed:
- General: Items that represent supplies that military men and women need: medical supplies, food, clothing, etc. They can be empty boxes and containers or cutouts created from cardboard.

Instructions:
- This is a relay race with two teams.
- Have the children line up and race to the other end of the raceway (the military zone) taking the supplies that are needed.
- They are to, one at a time, take one of the supplies to the military zone.
- When they return and tag the next child in line, that child then runs to take another needed item to the military zone.
- The team that has taken the items to the zone and returned first wins the game.

Chapter 3
True Trust

Grace and TJ with their Sweet Trust flowers

Trashing Trust
Discussion: "Trashing Trust" discusses what trust is, trusting people, and trusting God.
Craft: Garden Seeds
Indoor Activity: Statues
Outdoor Activity: Blind Trust

Feelings and Trust
Discussion: "Feelings and Trust" discusses trusting God when things happen that we don't like.
Craft: Trusting Jesus Flag
Indoor Activity: The Level Game
Outdoor Activity: Finding Your Way

Pure Trust
Discussion: "Pure Trust" explains what something is when it is pure and further explains the purity of God's Word.
Craft: Father's Coupons
Indoor Activity: Fluttering Flowers
Outdoor Activity: God's World Hike

Trusting Praise
Discussion: When trusting that all good things come from God, we offer Him praise, love, and honor in return.
Craft: Sweet Trust
Indoor Activity: Praise Shakers
Outdoor Activity: Picnic Theater

Chapter 3: True Trust

Devotional Doodles
Draw a Picture
Draw a picture of something that grows.

How Many

words can you make using these letters
FAITH AND TRUST

_____   _____
_____   _____
_____   _____
_____   _____
_____   _____
_____   _____
_____   _____
_____   _____
_____   _____
_____   _____

Find the Words

V	K	H	J	E	S	U	S	F	E
G	L	P	R	A	Y	E	R	A	F
H	O	L	Y	S	P	I	R	I	T
T	A	D	H	U	B	N	T	T	H
R	I	E	L	S	I	E	H	H	W
U	T	S	S	R	B	J	N	B	A
S	R	G	B	E	L	I	E	V	E
T	E	R	I	S	E	I	A	B	T
P	U	R	E	U	T	H	E	R	E
R	S	D	A	T	K	M	G	E	R

TRUST   FAITH   HOLY SPIRIT
BIBLE   PURE   JESUS
PRAYER   GOD   BELIEVE

Trashing Trust

Prior to Discussion
- Have a Bible available and ask for volunteers to read.

Discussion
Ask: *Allow time for discussion.*
- What is trust?

Say:
- Trust is being able to completely rely on someone or something.
- It is being certain or confident.

Ask: *Allow time for discussion.*
- Why do you think trust may or may not be important?
- How can you help people trust you?
- Is being trustworthy, or being someone who can be trusted, important to you?
- Do you do things to help people trust you?
- Do you trust yourself?

Say:
- Many Bible scholars believe that wise King Solomon wrote this proverb:

Read: Proverbs 28:26

Ask: *Allow time for discussion.*
- What does this mean?
- When we are struggling with anything, should we do whatever we think is right or should we get advice and guidance from God?

Say:
- As Christians, we know that our Lord knows what is best for us.
- We need to be wise and trust Him more than we trust ourselves.

Ask: *Allow time for discussion.*
- Are there people in your life that you trust?
- Do you believe they will always want "the best" for you?
- Do you trust them completely and totally?
- Do you think these people could make mistakes and do things that may harm your trust?

Say:
- All people make mistakes and do things that they shouldn't.
- The Bible does say that we are all sinners.

Read: Romans 3:23

Say:
- Sometimes people will let us down but God will never let us down.
- He never makes mistakes and He is never wrong.
- Listen to what King David wrote:

Read: Psalm 118:8

Say:
- Every human makes mistakes and does things that shouldn't be done.
- King David is saying that we should put our trust and confidence in God more than any human.

Ask: *Allow time for discussion.*
- Does this mean that we should not trust our parents, grandparents, or friends?

Say:
- It means that we should trust God more than anyone else.

Ask: *Allow time for discussion.*
- If someone tells you something that is the opposite of what God says, who is always right?
- If someone says something about God that is opposite of what is in the Bible, what would you think?

Say:
- We know beyond a shadow of a doubt that we can trust God.
- Trusting ourselves or others more than God is throwing your trust away.
- Some scholars believe that Paul wrote the book of Hebrews: the letter written to Hebrew believers.

Read: Hebrews 10:35

Final Thought:
Throughout the Bible and in this letter, the writers tell believers that we should not throw away our confidence and trust. Wisdom is putting our trust in our Lord above all else.

Chapter 3: True Trust

Trashing Trust — Activities

Craft: Garden Seeds
Items Needed:
- General: Newspapers and Potting Soil
- Per Child: 1 Paper Towel, 1 Apron, 1 Coffee Filter, 1 Plant Pot, and Plant Seeds

Butterfly-Attracting Plants:
Artemisias, Asters, Black-Eyed Susans, Butterfly Bushes, Buttonbushes, Coreopsis, Daisies, Dandelions, Mallows, Mints, Passionflowers, Privets, Queen Anne's Lace, Red Clover, Self-Heal, Sweet Peas, Verbenas, Vetches, and Violets.

Instructions:
- Have the children put on aprons to protect their clothing.
- Put newspaper on the table for easier cleanup.
- Give each child a plant pot and a coffee filter.
- The coffee filter will be placed into the pot to line the bottom and keep the dirt inside the pot.
- Soil will be placed on top of the coffee filter, filling up the pot about three fifths of the way.
- Have them poke a hole in the soil to put the seeds in. (The hole should be approximately four times larger than the size of the seeds, but read the package directions for specific instructions.)
- Give each child some seeds and have them put their seeds in the hole in the soil.
- Tape a paper towel over the top of each pot so they can carry the pots without spilling the soil, and tell them to take it off when they get the plants home.
- Remind the children to water the plants.
- While they are working, open a discussion about trusting God with our gardens and that only God can make seeds sprout and plants grow.

Variation:
- This can be done as a group garden that the children will care for each week.

Indoor Activity: Statues
Instructions:
- Explain that we can stand around like statues, or we can work toward completing God's purpose for our lives.
- Children will stand in a circle.
- The leader will call out "your job is to . . ." and fill in different actions.
- The children will perform the action until the leader calls out, "Your job is to freeze!"
- All of the children will freeze and stand like a statue.
- The leader will call out different actions and freeze intermittently.
- If a child moves when he or she should be frozen, that child is out of the game.
- The last child to follow the commands completely wins the game.

Outdoor Activity: Blind Trust
Items Needed:
- Per Team: Play Dough and 1 Blindfold

Instructions:
- Assemble teams of two to three children and give each team one blindfold.
- Each team will choose the "truster" who will wear the blindfold.
- The leader will call out an object that each team will create with the play dough.
- The blindfolded "truster" will use play dough to create the object.
- Team members will guide the "truster" in creating the object.
- The first team to complete the object wins the game.

Page 26 — Christian Living

Feelings and Trust

Prior to Discussion
- Have a Bible available and ask for volunteers to read.

Discussion
Ask: *Allow time for answers.*
- What is trust?

Say:
- Trust is being able to completely rely on someone or something.
- It is being certain or confident.

Ask: *Allow time for discussion.*
- Who can we always trust? *Guide them to God, Jesus, and the Holy Spirit.*

Say:
- It is wise to trust God more than we trust anyone or anything.

Ask: *Allow time for discussion.*
- Is it easy to trust God when we are happy with our lives?
- Do you think it is easy to trust God when He is answering our prayers by giving us what we ask for?
- Do you think it is just as easy to trust God if your parent is dying and God is not healing your parent and making him or her get better?
- Do you think it might be hard to trust God when things are not going the way you want them to?

Say:
- We can always trust that God knows what He is doing.
- God never said, "You have to like everything that I do."
- God never said, "You have to understand everything that I do."
- God does want us to accept all that He does, trusting that He really does know what is best.

Ask: *Allow time for discussion.*
- If you saw a little boy running after his ball into the road and you saw a car coming, would you stop the boy from running into the road?
- Would you help the boy even if he gets mad at you because the car ran over his ball and popped it?
- How would you feel if he started crying about his ball?

Say:
- It may make us feel bad for the little boy, even though stopping him was what he needed.
- God doesn't like stopping us from doing things or avoiding giving us what we want.
- God doesn't enjoy it when you are sad that a family member or friend dies, especially when you have prayed He would heal them.
- He does know what is best though.
- Listen to Jesus' words.

Read: John 14:1

Say:
- While in prison, Paul wrote a letter to encourage the Philippian church.
- He wanted them to see where joy comes from.

Read: Philippians 4:6

Say:
- King David wrote about trusting God as well.

Read: Psalm 62:8

Say:
- Think about that little boy again.
- His ball is ruined and he is unhappy.
- Maybe he doesn't understand how anything good could have come from this.
- He may even blame you for his ball being ruined.
- It is likely that he is not even thinking that you saved his life.

Final Thought:
We are like this with God at times. Things happen that we don't like and we get angry or upset, we blame God for allowing it, and we may even cry. God may feel bad because He loves us, but He always knows what is best. We can always trust Him even if things are not going the way we want them to.

Feelings and Trust — Activities

Chapter 3: True Trust

Craft: Trusting Jesus Flag

Items Needed:
- General: Crayons or Markers, Scrap Paper, Miscellaneous Decorations, Glue, and Tape
- Per Child: 1 Paint Stirrer and 1 Sheet of Construction Paper

Instructions:
- Give each child a sheet of construction paper and tell them that these will be their flags.
- They will use the supplies to decorate their flags in a way that will represent trusting Jesus.
- They will each tape their flag to a paint stirrer, so they can wave their flags to show others that they trust Jesus.

Indoor Activity: The Level Game

Items Needed:
- General: Water, Glue, and Colorful Paper Scraps
- Per Child: 3 2-Liter Bottles and 1 Ball

Instructions:
- The children will use the paper scraps to decorate each bottle.
- To play the game with their family and friends, they will leave one bottle empty, fill one bottle half full, and fill one bottle completely.
- Using the ball, they will try to knock over all three bottles.
- While they are working, open a discussion about which bottle will be the hardest to knock over and whether being filled with trust in God makes us stand stronger and steadier for God.

If There's Time:
Have a game set for the children to play while the glue is drying.

Outdoor Activity: Finding Your Way

Items Needed:
- General: Paper, Pencils, and Crayons or Markers
- Per Team: 4 Index Cards

Instructions
- Divide the children into teams of two to four children.
- Have each team draw a map of the yard, drawing landmarks such as buildings, gardens, and trees.
- Each team will write one clue on each index card to help find other hidden clues.
- One at a time, each team will hide three index cards based on the clues.
- When all teams have hidden the cards, the teams will swap the remaining card and the map with another team.
- When the leader says "GO" the teams will use the map and the clue on the card to find a card, which they will use to find another, and so on.
- The first team to collect all of the cards wins the game.
- While the children are working on the maps and clues, open a discussion about trusting God to guide us on our life's journey.

Variation:
- Leader can create maps and clues for children.

Chapter 3: True Trust

Pure Trust

Prior to Discussion
- Have a Bible available and ask for volunteers to read.
- Have a bowl, a spoon, a small amount of sugar, and food coloring available.
- (Optional) Have a video of refining silver available. Video on YouTube by G&S Metals and Refiners. Scan QR code or go to: www.youtube.com/watch?v=l3BuUJJOCA4 to view.

Discussion
Say:
- Trust is being able to completely rely on someone or something.

Ask: *Allow time for discussion.*
- What comes to your mind when I say **PURE TRUST**?
- What does pure mean?

Say:
- If something is pure, there is nothing else mixed with it.
- It is what it is.
- I'm going to show you an example.

Action:
- Show the children the sugar.

Ask: *Allow time for answers.*
- What do you know about sugar?
- What happens to sugar if we mix it with food coloring?

Action:
- Mix the food coloring and sugar together.

Ask: *Allow time for answers.*
- Is the sugar still pure?

Say:
- Pure sugar is absolutely and only sugar.
- There are people who refine silver to make it pure.
- They heat the silver to a very high temperature so everything else burns away and only the silver remains.

Action (optional):
- Let children view the video.

Say:
- So, when silver is pure, it is absolutely and only silver.

Ask: *Allow time for answers.*
- Did you know that words can be pure as well?

Say:
- Pure words are absolutely and only what is said.
- Listen to King David describing God's words.

Read: Psalm 3:16
Say:
- He is comparing God's words to pure silver.
- Everything that God speaks has nothing that is wrong or bad or untrue.
- His words are like silver that is refined so everything that is not silver is burned away; it is only and absolutely silver.
- His words can be trusted.
- We can purely trust each and every word of His.
- God wants us to understand and remember that what He says will happen.

Read: Isaiah 55:11
Say:
- Isaiah is saying that, if God says it, you can always count on it.
- In a letter to the Roman Christians, Paul mentioned Abraham's trust in God's words.

Read: Romans 4:21-22
Say:
- God had told Abraham he would have a child.
- Abraham believed God's words, even though he and his wife were too old to have children.

Final Thought:
This is the kind of trust we can have in God's words as well. If God says it, we can purely trust each word. He only says what He means. We can completely rely on God and we can be certain and confident on every pure word that He has ever spoken.

Pure Trust — Activities

Chapter 3: True Trust

Craft: Father's Coupons
Items Needed:
- General: Poster Board, Stapler, Scissors, and Crayons or Markers
- Per Child: 1/2 Sheet of Construction Paper and 2 Sheets of White Copy Paper

Instructions:
- Open a discussion about things children can do for their dads to make them feel loved and appreciated.
- Write their ideas on the poster board so they can use the ideas for their coupon books.
- Have each child cut the 1/2 sheet of construction paper in half. This will be the front and back covers for the coupon book.
- Have each child cut the two pieces of white paper in half and then cut those in half, so they have 4 pieces from each sheet of white paper, 8 total.
- They will put the sheets together with the construction paper on the outside and staple on one edge to create a booklet.
- On the outside of the booklet, ask them to write "Dad's Coupon Book."
- Inside their booklets, they will create coupons for things they will do for their dads when asked.
- On the back of each coupon, they will write one of the fruits of the Spirit that we can all practice for our Heavenly Father.
- Dad can tear out the coupon and redeem it when he wants that particular thing done.

Indoor Activity: Fluttering Flowers
Items Needed:
- General: Newspapers, Potting Soil, and Water in Container
- Per Child: 1 Paper Towel, 1 Apron, 1 Coffee Filter, Small Plant Pot, and 1 Plant

Butterfly-Attracting Plants:
Artemisias, Asters, Black-Eyed Susans, Butterfly Bushes, Buttonbushes, Coreopsis, Daisies, Dandelions, Mallows, Mints, Passionflowers, Privets, Queen Anne's Lace, Red Clover, Self-Heal, Sweet Peas, Verbenas, Vetches, and Violets.

Instructions:
- Have the children put on aprons to protect their clothing.
- Put newspaper on the table for easier cleanup.
- Give each child a plant pot and a coffee filter.
- The coffee filter will be placed into the pot to line the bottom and keep the dirt inside the pot.
- Soil will be placed on top of the coffee filter, filling up the pot about three fifths of the way.
- Have them dig a hole in the soil and place the plant in the pot.
- Cover the plant's roots and pat down the soil.
- Tell the children to remember to give their plants some water.
- While they are working, open a discussion about trusting God's plans, even for butterflies.

Outdoor Activity: God's World Hike
Items Needed:
- General: Markers
- Per Child: 1 Paper Lunch Bag

Instructions:
- Give each child a bag, and tell them to write their names on their bags.
- Take a hike around the yard.
- The children will find items that God created and put them in their bags.
- After the hunt, they will show the other children their items.
- Have the children discuss why God may have created each item.
- During the hike, open a discussion about trusting that all of God's creations are great.

Trusting Praise

Prior to Discussion
- Have a Bible available and ask for volunteers to read.

Discussion
Ask: *Allow time for discussion.*
- What is praise?

Say:
- Praise is a way to express admiration, appreciation, awe, honor, love, and respect.

Ask: *Allow time for discussion.*
- Has someone ever told you, "Good job!"?
- Have you ever received an award for doing some outstanding thing?
- Have you ever told someone, "Thank you!"?
- What are some other ways that we can show others that they are appreciated, respected, honored, loved, and admired?
- What are some ways that we can praise God?
- Did you know that people throughout the Bible praised God in many different ways?

Say:
- We can praise Him through songs like Moses did after God parted the Red Sea to save him and the Israelites.

Read: Exodus 15:1
Say:
- David praised God in a song when God saved him when Saul was trying to kill him.

Read: 2 Samuel 22:1
Say:
- After King Solomon dedicated the temple, they praised God with instruments that King David made specifically for praising the Lord.

Read: 2 Chronicles 7:5-6
Say:
- When we truly trust God, Jesus, and The Holy Spirit, we know where our blessings come from.
- We are so thankful that we want to give praise to our Lord and King.
- King David gives us an additional way to praise Him.

Read: Psalm 9:11
Read: Psalm 109:30
Say:
- We can praise Him by telling others what He has done.
- By telling others about our Lord and our blessings, we are praising Him.
- King David wrote a lot about praising the Lord.
- In one of his Psalms, he mentions many ways to praise Him.

Read: Psalm 150:1-6
Final Thought:

We can praise God in many different ways, and we can have fun and enjoy praising Him. Choosing a way to praise Him is not as important as taking time to do it. The important thing is that we let Him know that we admire, appreciate, honor, love, and respect Him.

Trusting Praise

Activities

Chapter 3: True Trust

Craft: Sweet Trust

Items Needed:
- General: Scissors, Crayons or Markers, Tape, and a Hole Puncher
- Per Child: Two 1/4 Sheets of Construction Paper (one green, the other a flower petal color) and a Sucker (Dum Dum suckers work well for this)

Instructions:
- Explain that they will be making gifts to give to people and begin a discussion about trusting Jesus.
- Give each child two 1/4 sheets of construction paper and a sucker.
- Each child will cut the non-green construction paper into the shape of a flower and decorate it.
- When they have finished decorating the flowers, they will each punch a hole in the center of the flower.
- They will each put a sucker into the center of the flower and tape it onto the bottom of the flower.
- The sucker is the stem of the flower.
- Tell them to use green construction paper and cut out leaf shapes to tape to the sucker stick (flower stem).
- While they are working, open a discussion about whom they will give the flower to and what they will tell him or her about trusting Jesus.

Variation:
- Each child can make a card to go with the Sweet Trust Sucker to give to a group such as home bound people or a fire department.

Indoor Activity: Praise Shakers

Items Needed:
- General: Bag of Dried Beans, Scissors, Tape, Markers or Crayons
- Per Child: 1/2 Sheet of Construction Paper, 1 Plastic Drink Bottle with Lid

Instructions:
- Give each child 1/2 sheet of construction paper, 1 plastic drink bottle, and some dried beans.
- Each child should decorate one side of the construction paper.
- Wrap the construction paper around the bottle (tape it so it will stay on the bottle).
- Place beans in the bottles, put the lids on, and they have shakers.
- Tell the children that they can use their shakers when they are singing praise songs to our Lord.

Let's Shake Game: *(if there is time)*
- The leader will call out the words: Believe, Faith, or Move.
- When Believe is called, the children will shake their shakers over their heads.
- When Faith is called, they will shake the shakers with their arms stretched out to their side.
- When Move is called, they will shake the shakers and move in silly ways until the next word is called out.

Outdoor Activity: Picnic Theater

Items Needed:
- General: Large old Blanket or Sheet (enough for everyone to sit on), Snacks, Drinks, Napkins, Markers or Crayons, Glue, and Miscellaneous Decorations
- Per Child: 1 Paper Lunch Bag

Puppet Instructions:
- Tell the children to sit on the blanket and give each child a paper lunch bag.
- The children will each create a paper bag puppet that can praise God.
- While they are working, open a discussion about reasons we have to praise God.

Theater Instructions:
- Give the children a napkin, snack, and drink.
- Divide the children into teams of two or three.
- Each team will use their puppets to put on a puppet show that praises God for different reasons.
- The children who are not performing will enjoy their snacks while watching the show.

Chapter 4
Spiritual Armor

Trinity with her Shield of Faith

What is Spiritual Armor?
Discussion: "What is Spiritual Armor?" tells children about the armor God has given us to help us live successfully as Christians.
Craft: Spiritual Armor Posters
Indoor Activity: Spiritual Armor Match Game
Outdoor Activity: Armor Relay

Truth and Righteousness
Discussion: "Truth and Righteousness" discusses what these two pieces of armor are and how they are used.
Craft: Righteousness Cupcakes
Indoor Activity: If You're Righteous . . .
Outdoor Activity: Hopping for Truth

Peace and Faith
Discussion: "Peace and Faith" discusses these two pieces of armor and how they are used and shared.
Craft: Shield of Faith
Indoor Activity: Magazine Hunt
Outdoor Activity: Paper Attack

Salvation and the Word
Discussion: "Salvation and the Word" discusses two very important pieces of armor and how they protect us.
Craft: Praise Bags
Indoor Activity: Carry the Armor
Outdoor Activity: Armor Holes Game

Prayer
Discussion: "Prayer" discusses the privilege and duty of Christians to take everything to God in prayer.
Craft: Prayer Board
Indoor Activity: Help Me Pray
Outdoor Activity: Temptation Tag

Chapter 4: Spiritual Armor

Devotional Doodles
Use the Shapes
Use the shapes to create a picture of your spiritual armor.

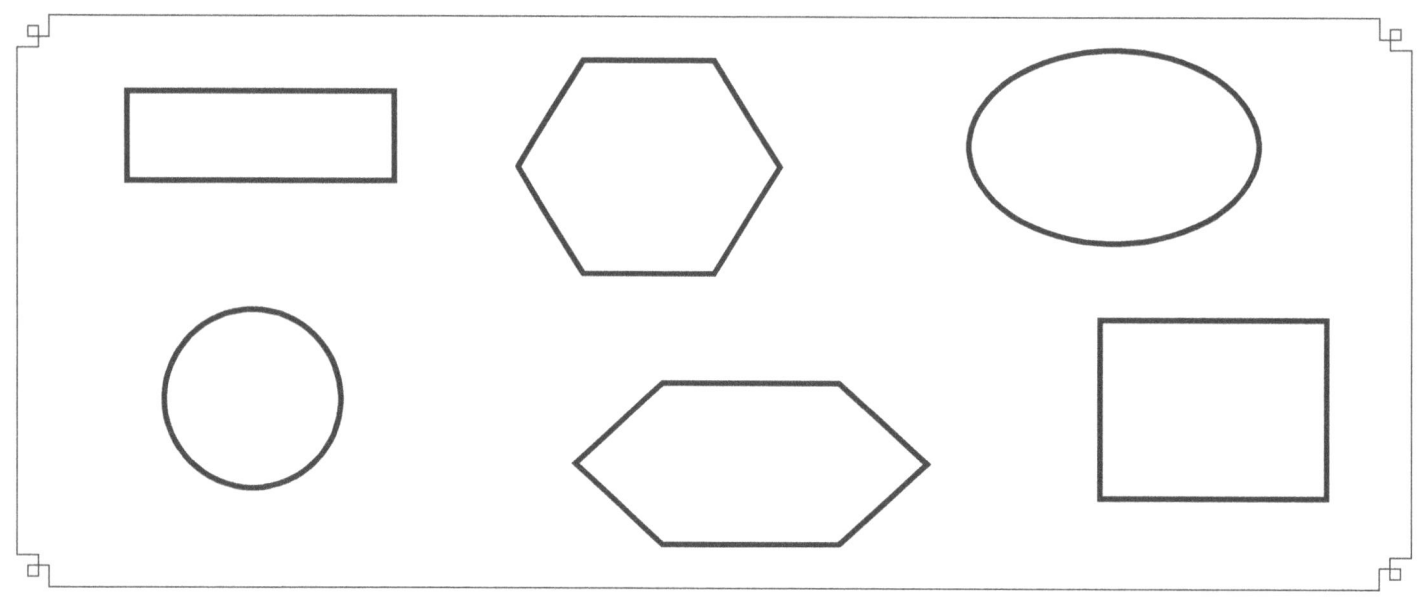

Find the Words

```
B R E T E N A W S T G H H T R
U R F D P R G G D E T E D O R
I E E Z H I D D O R L R O G O
M A G A E G S O U M O M U L M
G S N Y S H F T E S O W A T R
N O F A I T H T X A R E L K A
I J E C A E P H D L E I H S L
Y H I E N O L L R V D L A S A
A N X I S U V K A A O N W E U
R C F F S S A L T T L E B N T
P W P S P N I P L I E P I I I
D T J I G E F M H O P J T D R
C D R O W S N N O N S S R A I
G I R H C S O T F G O D I E P
T Y N E E T H G I E G F X R S
```

EASY WORD LIST
EPHESIANS
SALVATION
TEN
GOD
BREASTPLATE
RIGHTEOUSNESS
FAITH

DIFFICULT WORD LIST
SPIRITUAL ARMOR
HELMET
SIX
SWORD
SPIRIT
EIGHTEEN
WORD
BELT
TRUTH
PRAYING
READINESS
GOSPEL
PEACE
SHIELD

Page 34   Christian Living

What is Spiritual Armor?

Prior to Discussion
- Have a Bible available and ask for volunteers to read.
- Have a white board and dry erase markers or chalk board and chalk
- You will need a copy of the Spiritual Armor cutouts. See Page 80.

Discussion
Ask: *Allow time for discussion.*
- What is armor and what is its purpose?
- Have you ever been knocked over by a large dog, because you didn't see it coming?
- Have you ever gone into the water at the beach and had a wave knock you over?

Say:
- If you see the dog coming or know the wave is strong, you can plant your feet more firmly and stand strong.
- Our spiritual armor helps us stand firm.
- In his letter, which became the book of Ephesians, Paul wrote about spiritual armor.

Read: Ephesians 6:10-11
Say:
- God gives us our spiritual armor to help us get through temptations and the desire to sin.
- With our spiritual armor we are better representatives for God.

Ask: *Allow time for answers.*
- Can you name any of the pieces of "the full armor of God" that Paul mentioned in Ephesians 6:13-17?

Action:
- Place the spiritual armor picture in a place where the children can see it.
- As you read the verses, write the names of the different pieces of armor on the chalk board or white board.

Read: Ephesians 6:13-17
Say:
- The pieces of armor are:
  - » the belt of truth
  - » the breastplate of righteousness
  - » the gospel of peace on your feet
  - » the shield of faith
  - » the helmet of salvation
  - » the sword of the Spirit (the Word)
- Paul wrote about the different pieces of armor.
- Each piece of armor represents things that our generous God gives us if we seek them.
- Our armor includes truth, righteousness, peace, faith, salvation, and His Word.

Ask: *Allow time for discussion.*
- Which one of these do you think is the most important in the life of a believer and why?

Say:
- Each of these pieces of armor are important, but the next verse in his letter explains the most important part of our Christian life.
- It is not something that we are given but something that is important for us to do.

Read: Ephesians 6:18
Say:
- All of our armor is great and we need each piece of it, but prayer is our communication with God and builds our relationship with our Lord and Savior.
- Prayer also helps build our armor.

Final Thought:
Each piece of our armor and prayer are important in our Christian life, and help us live our life for Jesus and become more like Him. Let's remember to put on our armor and diligently serve God.

Chapter 4: Spiritual Armor

What is Spiritual Armor? — Activities

Craft: Spiritual Armor Posters
Items Needed:
- General: Poster Boards, Tape, Crayons or Markers, Miscellaneous Decorations, Old Magazines, Glue, Construction Paper, Pencils, Erasers, and Scissors
- Per Child: 1 Sheet of White Paper and 1 Poster Board

Instructions:
- Give each child a poster board.
- Tell them to use the white paper to draw what they want, make changes, and get it as close to perfect as they can.
- When they each know how they are going to put it on their poster, they will use their white paper drawings as a guide to put their creations on the poster boards.
- Each child should write the title "Spiritual Armor" on his or her poster.
- They will each decorate their posters with magazine cutouts, drawings, images, and words to create a Roman Soldier.
- Have the children draw each piece of spiritual armor on the soldier.
- When they have finished their posters, each child will tell everyone about his or her poster.
- Each child will find a special spot on the wall to decorate the room with his or her poster.

Craft: Spiritual Armor Posters
Long-Term Project
- Each of the next three discussions will cover two of the spiritual armor pieces.
- After each piece of armor is discussed, allow the children to add that piece to their poster.
- Each child will need a copy of the Soldier cutout. See Page 79.
- Each child will need a copy of the Spiritual Armor cutouts. See Page 80.
- See page 78 for a sample of the poster craft.

See Page 77 for Craft Sample

Indoor Activity: Spiritual Armor Match Game
Items Needed:
- General: Crayons or Markers, Miscellaneous Decorations, Glue, Construction Paper, Scissors
- Per Child: 6 Index Cards

Instructions:
- Give each child six index cards and explain that they will each create their very own Spiritual Armor Match Game.
- They will cut each index card in half.
- Using the art supplies, they will draw two images of each piece of spiritual armor.
- See Ephesians 6:13-17 for spiritual armor.
- There will be two duplicates of each piece of armor.

If There is Time:
- Have a game set so they can play the game while their games are drying.

Playing the Game:
- To play the game, they will place all of the game pieces on a table with the images facing down. Each player take turns turning over two pieces to find the matches. If the player finds a match, they try again. If the player doesn't find a match, it is the next player's turn.

Outdoor Activity: Armor Relay
Instructions:
- This is a relay race that will utilize some of their "spiritual armor."
- Divide the children into two teams.
- One at a time, the children will race with their SHOES to the relay line where a leader is located.
- When the child gets to the relay line, he or she will tell the leader a SWORD (Bible) verse (or something that they know about the Bible) before running back with their SHOES to the starting line.
- When a child crosses the starting line, the next child may take his or her turn.
- The team that has all members back to the starting line first wins.
- If a child is having trouble thinking of a verse, the other children on their team should help him or her by sharing God's Word.

Truth and Righteousness

Prior to the Discussion
- Have a Bible available and ask for volunteers to read.
- You will need a copy of the Spiritual Armor Cutouts. See Page 80.

Discussion
Ask: *Allow time for comments.*
- Can you name some of the pieces of the spiritual armor mentioned in Ephesians 6:13-18?

Say:
- They are:
    » the belt of truth
    » the breastplate of righteousness
    » the gospel of peace on your feet
    » the shield of faith
    » the helmet of salvation
    » the sword of the Spirit (the Word)
- We are going to talk about two pieces of the armor today: the belt and the breastplate.

Read: Ephesians 6:14

Action:
- Place the Spiritual Armor picture in a place where the children can see it.

Say:
- Our spiritual armor helps us stand firm in God's will for us and against whatever comes our way.
- The first piece of armor is the belt of truth.

Ask: *Allow time for comments.*
- What do you think the belt of truth is?

Read: John 14:6

Say:
- Truth is from God and He sent Jesus to be His truth.
- Jesus is the true way to salvation and the way to have a close relationship with God.
- Truth is God's words; everything He says is true!
- The Bible, which is God's Word, contains God's truth.

Ask: *Allow time for discussion.*
- Can you tell me a truth from the Bible?
- What truth do you know about Adam and Eve?
- What truth does the Bible teach about Daniel's devotion to God?
- Can you tell me the truth about Jesus?
- Do you know anything about the truth of receiving salvation through Jesus?

Ask: *Allow time for answers.*
- How do we find out God's truth? *Steer them toward the Bible, parents, teachers, preachers, and prayer.*

Say:
- The next piece of armor is the breastplate of righteousness.

Ask: *Allow time for answers.*
- What can you tell me about this?
- What does it mean when God wipes out our sins?

Say:
- It means we are made righteous.

Ask: *Allow time for answers.*
- If you know God washed away your sins, would you feel good about yourself?
- Do you believe your relationship with God would be closer?
- So, how can we have this righteousness?

Say:
- Our righteousness comes through our faith in Jesus and our turning away from our sins.

Final Thought:

Truth and righteousness are the first two pieces of armor that Paul mentions in his letter to the Ephesian church. Knowing God's truth and our righteousness through Jesus helps us combat temptations, wrong thoughts, and being led away from God. God loves us and has given us help to stand firm in His will.

Chapter 4: Spiritual Armor

Truth and Righteousness — Activities

Craft: Righteousness Cupcakes
Items Needed:
- General: Icing and Decorations, Plates, Napkins, Cups, and Something to Drink
- Per Child: 2 Snacks (cupcakes or cookies)

Instructions:
- Explain that they will each decorate one snack to give away, so they can explain righteousness to whoever receives it.
- The second one is for them to celebrate the truth, or Good News, of the Gospel.
- Give each child a drink, a plate, a napkin, two snacks, and some decorations.
- The children will decorate the snacks in a way that represents righteousness.
- While they are working, invite the children to practice telling someone about the snack.

Craft: Spiritual Armor Posters
Long-Term Project

Items Needed:
- General: Crayons or Markers, Glue, Construction Paper, and Scissors
- Poster from "What is Spiritual Armor?" discussion

Instructions:
- Each child will need a copy of the Soldier cutout. See Page 79.
- Each child will need a copy of the Spiritual Armor cutouts. See Page 80.
- The children will create and add the belt and the breastplate to their Roman soldier poster.
- They will write the part of our Christian life with which the armor goes.

Indoor Activity: If You're Righteous . . .
Instructions:
- Have the children stand in a circle.
- To the tune of "If You're Happy and You Know It," sing the words "If you're righteous and you know it," adding words of different actions that the children can do.
- Have each child in the circle take turns saying an action that everyone should do.
- Examples: If you're righteous and you know it clap your hands, ... jump up and down, ... pat your head, ... say, "I love God."

Variation:
- Have the children perform each action that was previously done in addition to the new one.

Outdoor Activity: Hopping for Truth
Items Needed:
- 2 Beanbags

Instructions:
- Divide the children into two teams and give each team a beanbag.
- Have each team stand in a circle.
- The child with the beanbag will hop around the outside of the circle and back to where he or she started.
- When the child returns to his or her spot, the child will hand the beanbag to the person on his or her right.
- When each child is handed the beanbag, it is his or her turn to hop around the circle.
- This will continue until all children have hopped around the circle.
- The winning team is the one whose members have all hopped around the circle and returned to their places first.

Variation:
- Other tasks: tossing the beanbag in the air and catching it, balancing it while doing a crab walk, walking backwards, skipping, hopping, etc.

Peace and Faith

Prior to Discussion
- Have a Bible available and ask for volunteers to read.
- You will need a copy of the Spiritual Armor cutouts. See Page 80.

Discussion
Ask: *Allow time for comments.*
- Can you name most of the pieces of spiritual armor mentioned in Ephesians 6:13-18?

Say:
- They are:
  » the belt of truth
  » the breastplate of righteousness
  » the gospel of peace on your feet
  » the shield of faith
  » the helmet of salvation
  » the sword of the Spirit (the Word)
- We are going to talk about two pieces of the armor today: the shoes and the shield.

Action:
- Place the Spiritual Armor picture in a place where the children can see it.

Say:
- Our spiritual armor helps us stand firm in our faith, get through temptations, and avoid being led away from God.
- The third piece of armor is our shoes.

Read: Ephesians 6:15
Ask: *Allow time for answers.*
- How can shoes represent peace?

Say:
- With our shoes on, we are ready to go.
- With God's peace, we are ready to move for God.
- He may ask you to reach other people with the Good News of Jesus.
- He may want you to share the peace that comes with the salvation and righteousness Jesus offers.
- God wants us to share this peace-making news with other people.
- He may want you to help a friend or neighbor.
- With God's peace, we are ready to move forward and right into His will.
- The next piece of armor is our shield of faith.

Read: Ephesians 6:16
Say:
- This verse says that the shield of faith "can extinguish all the flaming arrows of the evil one."

Ask: *Allow time for answers.*
- What does that mean and who is the evil one? *The evil one is Satan or the Devil.*

Say:
- The devil is able to send thoughts to our minds.
- These thoughts may cause us worry or may scare us.
- Putting up our shield of faith will combat the thoughts just like a shield will repel arrows.
- By having faith in God and placing our trust in Him, He becomes our shield.

Read: Proverbs 30:5
Ask: *Allow time for answers.*
- How can we increase our faith?

Say:
- When we read the Bible, sing, worship, and pray, our shield of faith grows stronger.

Final Thought:
God's peace and our faith are two important parts of our spiritual armor. These pieces help us stand firm in our beliefs. They also help combat temptation, wrong thoughts, and being led away from God. Our armor helps us stay in God's will.

Chapter 4: Spiritual Armor

Peace and Faith — Activities

Craft: Shield of Faith
Items Needed:
- General: Stapler, Crayons or Markers
- Per Child: 1/2 Sheet of Poster Board

Instructions:
- Give each child 1/2 sheet of poster board.
- Have the children cut a 1-inch strip from the bottom of the poster board. This will be the handle.
- Cut the corners of the poster board to make an oval shape. Younger children may need help with this.
- Have the children decorate the poster board to look like a shield.
- Ask the children to fold the 1-inch strip in half long ways to make it stronger.
- Staple the 1-inch strip to the edges of the poster board to create a handle. It can be drawn tighter to curve the shield. Use a few staples for each side to make it sturdier.

Craft: Spiritual Armor Posters
Long-Term Project

Items Needed:
- General: Crayons or Markers, Glue, Construction Paper, and Scissors
- Poster from "What is Spiritual Armor?" discussion

Instructions:
- Each child will need a copy of the Soldier cutout. See Page 79.
- Each child will need a copy of the Spiritual Armor cutouts. See Page 80.
- The children will create and add the shoes and the shields to their Roman soldier poster.
- They will write the part of our Christian life with which the armor goes.

Indoor Activity: Magazine Hunt
Items Needed:
- General: Magazines
- Per Child: 1 Sheet of Paper, 1 Pencil or Pen, Scissors, and Glue

Instructions:
- Choose a word or phrase from the discussion, for example: Jesus, Peace, Faith, Shield, Shoes, Bible, God's Word, etc.
- Give each child the supplies.
- Give the children a certain amount of time to look through magazines and find pictures that begin with each letter of the word or phrase.
- The child with the most pictures wins the game.

Variation:
- This may be done in teams.

Outdoor Activity: Paper Attack
Items Needed:
- Scrap Paper and Shields (from Shield of Faith craft), a Paper Notebook, or Paperback Book

Instructions:
- The children will write one temptation on each scrap piece of paper and ball it up.
- Divide the children into two teams.
- Each team will throw their temptation balls at the other team while blocking the incoming temptation balls with their shields.
- If a child gets hit with a paper ball, he or she is out.
- The last team to have people still playing wins.
- After the game, tell them that the team that picks up the most paper balls wins.

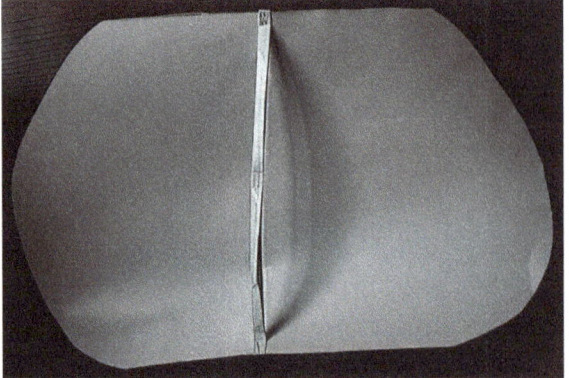

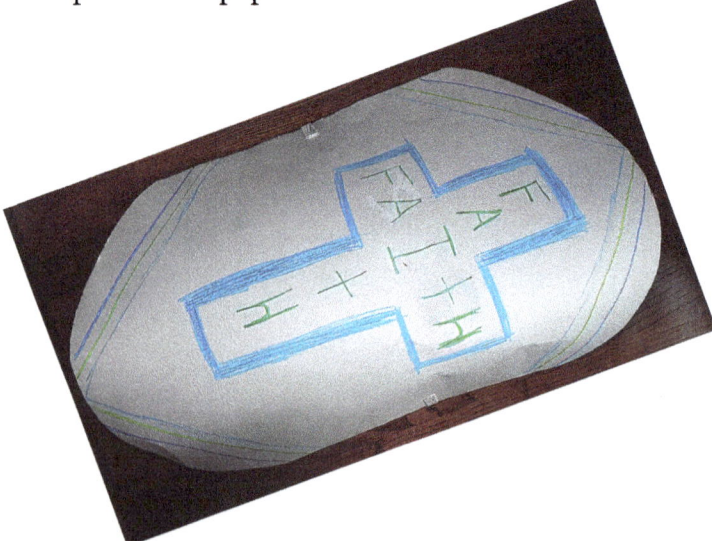

Chapter 4: Spiritual Armor

Salvation and the Word

Prior to Discussion
- Have a Bible available and ask for volunteers to read.
- You will need a copy of the Spiritual Armor cutouts. See Page 80.

Discussion
Ask: *Allow time for comments.*
- Can you name all of the pieces of spiritual armor that are mentioned in Ephesians 6:13-18?

Say:
- They are:
  » the belt of truth
  » the breastplate of righteousness
  » the gospel of peace on your feet
  » the shield of faith
  » the helmet of salvation
  » the sword of the Spirit (the Word)
- Today we are covering the last two: the helmet and the sword.

Read: Ephesians 6:17

Action:
- Place the Spiritual Armor picture in a place where the children can see it.

Say:
- The fifth piece of armor is the helmet of salvation.

Ask: *Allow time for discussion.*
- How do we receive salvation?

Say:
- We receive salvation through our faith in Jesus.

Read: John 3:16

Say:
- Faith and salvation work together.
- The final piece of armor is the sword of the Spirit.

Ask: *Allow time for answers*
- Who knows what this is? *Steer them toward the Bible.*
- Did you know that this is what Jesus used when Satan tried to tempt Him?

Read: Matthew 4:1-11

Say:
- When Jesus was tempted by Satan, Jesus quoted Scripture to show Satan that he was wrong.

Ask: *Allow time for discussion.*
- Have you ever been tempted?
- Can you think of any verses that may combat the temptation?

Say:
- Satan can put thoughts in our mind and we need to know when to reject them.
- Someone we know may try to tempt us.

Ask: *Allow time for discussion.*
- If someone tells you that it is okay to be mean to people who are mean to you, what would you say if you used the Bible to help you answer?
- What would be your response if someone said it is okay to take just one piece of candy from the store without paying for it?

Say:
- God's Word helps us combat anything that goes against God's will.
- The Bible is a very important part of our spiritual armor!
- The Bible reveals God's truth and brings us to righteousness, peace, faith, and salvation.
- All of our armor works together.
- The Word grows peace.
- Truth builds faith.
- Salvation brings righteousness.

Final Thought:
The pieces of armor that God has given us are useful for many things. Jesus was tempted by Satan and His spiritual armor was in place and helped Him. Our armor helps us stand firm for God when we are tempted or led away from Him.

Salvation and the Word — Activities

Chapter 4: Spiritual Armor

Craft: Praise Bags
Items Needed:
- General: Crayons or Markers, Staples, Dried Beans
- Per Child: 1/2 Sheet of Construction Paper

Instructions:
- Give each child 1/2 sheet of construction paper and some beans.
- Have the children decorate the construction paper, which will become their Praise Bags.
- Have the children fold their construction paper in half and staple the two sides together.
- Through the open top, have the children put some beans inside the construction paper.
- Have them staple the open top of the construction paper.
- Tell the children that they can use their Praise Bags as shakers while singing praise songs to God, or they can use their Praise Bag to play games with their friends.

Craft: Spiritual Armor Posters
Long-Term Project

Items Needed:
- General: Crayons or Markers, Glue, Construction Paper, and Scissors
- Poster from "What is Spiritual Armor?" discussion

Instructions:
- Each child will need a copy of the Soldier cutout. See Page 79.
- Each child will need a copy of the Spiritual Armor cutouts. See Page 80.
- The children will create and add the helmet and the sword to their Roman soldier poster.
- They will write the part of our Christian life with which the armor goes.

Indoor Activity: Carry the Armor
Items Needed: 1 Beanbag

Instructions:
- Have the children stand in a circle, and give one child the beanbag.
- The child with the beanbag will place the beanbag on his or her head and walk around the outside of the circle and back to where he or she started.
- When the child returns to his or her spot, the beanbag will be passed to the person on the right.
- When a child receives the beanbag, he or she will take a turn going around the circle.
- If the beanbag drops off a child's head, he or she is out of the game.
- The winner is the last child in the circle.

Variation:
- Other Tasks: tossing the beanbag in the air and catching it, balancing it while doing a crab walk, walking backwards, skipping, hopping, etc.

Outdoor Activity: Armor Holes Game
Items Needed:
- Per Child: Markers or Crayons, 6 Beanbags, 1 Box (large enough to cut 6 holes in the bottom that a beanbag will easily fit through)

Instructions:
- Cut six holes in the bottom of the box.(large enough for a beanbag to easily fit through).
- Cut the top off the box diagonally, so the open end of the box will be flat on the ground and the bottom will be slanted toward a player.
- Under each hole write one of the physical pieces of spiritual armor, and on each beanbag write one of the parts of our Christian life that it represents.
- Using the supplies, the children will decorate their boxes.

Playing the Game:
- Each child will take a turn tossing the beanbags into one of the armor holes in the box.
- The player earns twenty points if the bag goes into the hole that goes with the part of our Christian life that is represented on the bag, or ten points if the bag goes into any other hole.
- The player with the most points wins the game.

Prayer

Prior to Discussion
- Have a Bible available and ask for volunteers to read.

Discussion

Ask: *Allow time for answers.*
- What is prayer?

Say:
- Prayer is a way to talk to our Father.

Read: 2 Chronicles 7:14-15

Say: *Read Slowly*
- So our part is to humble ourselves, pray, seek His face, and turn from our wicked ways.
- His part is that He will hear, forgive our sins, and heal our land.
- Humble prayer and seeking His will brings with it God listening to us, forgiving us, and healing our land.
- Paul gave us some prayer advice in his letter to the Ephesian church.

Read: Ephesians 6:18

Say:
- That means all of the time!

Ask: *Allow time for discussion.*
- Do you think you could use up all of your prayers by praying all of the time?
- Do we only have a certain number of prayers?

Say:
- God doesn't limit the number of prayers; we can humbly go to our Father any time and all of the time, and He will hear us.
- Paul wrote that believers need to be alert and always keep on praying for all the saints.
- This means that believers need to pray for other believers.
- Paul advises believers to pray all of the time, but he also advises us to pray about everything.

Read: Philippians 4:6

Say:
- Paul continues his advice on prayer by example.
- Paul asked for prayer for himself.

Read: Ephesians 6:19

Ask: *Allow time for discussion.*
- What were Paul's prayer needs?

Say:
- He wanted The Holy Spirit to speak for him, to give him the words.
- He also wanted to be **fearless and bold** in sharing the gospel.

Ask: *Allow time for discussion.*
- What might Paul have had to fear?

Say:
- One of the reasons Paul was in prison was for saying that the salvation of Jesus was for all people, even non-Jewish people.
- Paul wrote Ephesians and three other letters (Philippians, Colossians, and Philemon) while he was in prison waiting to appeal the case against him.
- These are called his prison letters.

Ask: *Allow time for discussion.*
- Are you going to ask for prayer for yourself the way Paul did?

Final Thought:

Paul shared a lot of advice and knowledge in his letter to the Ephesian church. He knew the power of prayer and that God's promises are true. He believed that all people can be righteous and receive salvation through Jesus. Paul's faith in Jesus was everything and He wanted everyone to know Jesus and trust Him. Remember to use your spiritual armor and prayer as you live your Christian Life.

Prayer — Activities

Chapter 4: Spiritual Armor

Craft: Prayer Board

Prior to Craft:
- Paint one side of each sheet of cardboard with chalkboard paint (the spray paint works well)

Items Needed:
- General: Chalkboard Paint, Newspaper, Paint Brushes, Water Cup (to rinse brushes), Craft Paint, Miscellaneous Decorations, Chalk, Craft Sticks, and Glue
- Per Child: 1 Sheet of Cardboard (empty cereal boxes work well for this), 2 Craft Magnets, and 1 Apron

Instructions:
- Have the children put on aprons and spread newspaper on the table.
- Give each child a sheet of cardboard, and have them each glue craft sticks around the edges of the cardboard to create a frame.
- They will use the craft paint and decorations to decorate their frames.
- Have each child glue a craft magnet to the back of his or her prayer board.
- Tell them to use their prayer boards to write down their prayers as a reminder to pray without ceasing.
- Open a discussion about other people seeing what they are praying for, especially if the prayer is for the person seeing the prayers.

Variation:
- String may be used, instead of magnets, to hang the frame.

Indoor Activity: Help Me Pray

Items Needed:
- Per Team: 1 Hole Puncher, Scissors, Pencil or Pen, Tissue Paper, Yarn, and 1 Sheet of Construction Paper

Instructions:
- Divide the children into teams of two or three.
- Each team will work together, but each team member must keep one hand behind his or her back during the activity.
- Each team will fold the construction paper, trace one team member's hand, cut out the two hands, punch holes along the edges of the hands, sew the two hands together on three sides with the yarn, stuff the hands with the tissue paper, and finish sewing the hands together.
- The first team to have their praying hands together wins the game.

Outdoor Activity: Temptation Tag

Prior to Game:
- Open a discussion about what temptation is.
- Explain this example: You are very hungry and your mom has said that dinner is almost ready and you cannot have any cookies. When she leaves the room, you might be tempted to get just one cookie out of the cookie jar.
- Ask if they think actually getting a cookie would turn the temptation into a sin.
- Explain that when we are tempted we can read the Bible to see what God expects of us and pray that God will help us get through the temptation.

Instructions:
- This is a tag game.
- Choose one child to be temptation (it) and chase the other children.
- When a child is tagged, he or she becomes temptation and tries to tag another child.
- Designate an area to be a base for children to run to and not be tagged.
- The base will be called "Word" or "Prayer."
- This activity assists them with understanding that reading the Bible and praying helps us withstand temptation.

Chapter 5
Praise

Nicholas, Noah, and Braden with their frames

What is Praise?
Discussion: "What is Praise" focuses on ways we can praise God and what it means.
Craft: Praise Story Board
Indoor Activity: A Story of Praise
Outdoor Activity: LetUS Praise Garden

Why Praise God?
Discussion: "Why Praise God" discusses showing God that we love Him and the change in attitude it brings about for us.
Craft: Praise Decorations
Indoor Activity: Alphabet Praise
Outdoor Activity: Bubble Praise

Fellowship & Praise
Discussion: "Fellowship and Praise" gives examples from the Bible of times when God's people came together to praise Him and what happened during these times.
Craft: Musical Praise
Indoor Activity: Praising Him
Outdoor Activity: Praise Circle

Praising God
Discussion: "Praising God" discusses where our focus should be for true praise.
Craft: Praising Him Frame
Indoor Activity: Remember to Praise
Outdoor Activity: Praise God Relay

Chapter 5: Praise

Devotional Doodles
Use the Letters
Use the letters to draw a picture of yourself praising God.

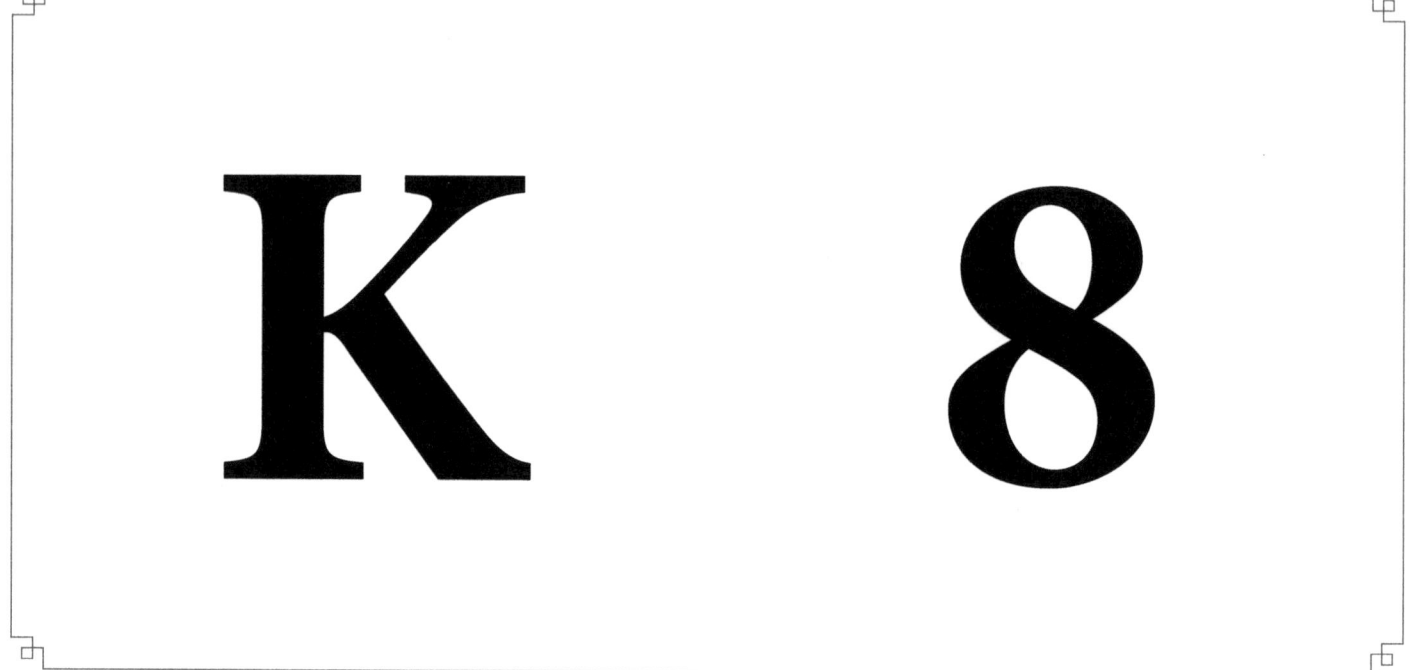

How Many
words can you make using these letters
PRAISING HIM

_____ _____
_____ _____
_____ _____
_____ _____
_____ _____
_____ _____
_____ _____
_____ _____
_____ _____

Find the Words

V	E	H	A	N	D	S	I	F	E
I	V	P	R	A	Y	S	N	A	F
H	E	L	P	R	A	I	S	E	S
T	R	D	H	D	B	N	T	T	O
R	Y	A	L	A	I	G	R	H	L
U	T	N	S	V	B	I	U	B	O
S	H	C	B	I	L	N	M	V	M
T	I	I	I	D	E	G	E	B	O
Z	N	N	F	A	T	H	N	R	N
R	G	G	B	R	E	A	T	H	R

PRAISES   DANCING   SOLOMON
SINGING   HANDS   EVERYTHING
INSTRUMENT   DAVID   BREATH

What is Praise?

Prior to Discussion
- Have a Bible available and ask for volunteers to read.

Discussion
Action:
- Complain about different things as the children arrive.
- Examples: the weather, the room, your clothing or hair, bugs, the amount of light in the room, etc.

Say:
- I was only pretending to be a grump and complain.

Ask: *Allow time for discussion.*
- How did my complaints make you feel?
- How do you think God feels when we are complaining and acting like a grump?
- Would it have been better if I had praised God instead of complaining?
- What is praise?

Say:
- Praise is showing approval, thankfulness, gratitude, and admiration.

Ask: *Allow time for answers.*
- Have you ever had someone praise you for doing a good job or for doing something for someone?
- What are some praises we could say to another person?

Say:
- Letting others know they are appreciated and that we are thankful for them is one way to love them.
- Listen to Paul's advice in his letter to Christians living in Rome.

Read: Romans 12:9-10
Say:
- Praise can also be done as a form of worship when the praise is focused on and directed toward God.
- Worshiping praise is a way to love God and thank Him for His blessings.
- Praise is usually connected to music of some type: songs, instruments, movements, etc.

Read: Psalm 30:4
Say:
- Praise can also be spoken words, letting God know that we love Him and thank Him for our blessings.
- Praise helps us focus our thoughts on God.

Read: Philippians 4:8
Ask: *Allow time for answers.*
- Is anything more praiseworthy than our Lord?

Final Thought:
Praise can be a song, words, playing an instrument, movements, etc. Praising God can help us overcome grumpiness and complaining. It helps focus our mind, heart, and spirit on God. Praise also lets God know that we love and appreciate Him. Let's remember to praise God each day, especially when we find ourselves complaining and being a grump.

What is Praise?

Activities

Craft: Praise Story Board
Items Needed:
- General: Felt, Craft Glue, and Scissors
- Per Child: Shoe Box

Instructions:
- Cover the inside of the box lid with a neutral colored piece of felt.
- The children will cut the felt into shapes to help tell a story of praise: people, animals, plants, stars, etc.
- While they are working, open a discussion about what they are creating.
- Using the figures, they will tell a story of praising God.
- The figures may be stored in the box while not in use.

Indoor Activity: A Story of Praise
Items Needed:
- Story Board from craft: (Praise Story Board)

Instructions:
- Each child will take a turn telling his or her praise story using the figures and box lid.

Outdoor Activity: LetUS Praise Garden
Items Needed:
- General: Tape, Newspaper, Potting Soil, and Water, Paint Brushes, Paint, and Cups of Water (to wash brushes)
- Per Child: Apron, Small Plant Pot, Coffee Filter, 1 Paper Towel, and Lettuce Seeds

Instructions:
- Have the children put on aprons.
- Put newspaper on the table and give each child a plant pot and a coffee filter.
- Using the paint, the children will write, "LetUS Praise Him" on the pot and decorate it.
- The coffee filter will be placed into the pot to line the bottom and keep the soil inside the pot.
- Soil will be placed on top of the coffee filter, filling up the pot about three fifths of the way.
- The children will scatter the seeds on the top of the soil. Follow the package directions for specific instructions.
- Tape a paper towel over the top of each pot so the children can carry the pots without spilling the soil.
- Explain that they will find a sunny home, take off the towel, and water the seeds.
- While they are working, open a discussion about praising God for the food that we can grow in our gardens.

Mission Project:
- This activity may be given to people in nursing homes and home-bound family and friends.

Chapter 5: Praise

Why Praise God?

Prior to Discussion
- Have a Bible available and ask for volunteers to read.
- Have some paper and pencils or pens available.
- Choose a song with an easy tune that the children know or can easily learn. *Example: This Old Man, Jesus Loves Me, etc.*

Discussion
Ask: *Allow time for discussion.*
- What are some reasons for us to praise God?

Say:
- Praise is taking time to show our love for God.
- Praise is thanking God for everything around us.
- It is letting Him know that we love the amazing things that He does for us.
- It is meditating on how good He is.

Read: Psalm 13:6
Say:
- Praise can be showing appreciation for Jesus.

Read: 1 Corinthians 15:57
Say:
- Praise can change our thoughts as we focus on our blessings.

Ask: *Allow time for answers.*
- Is it possible to praise God and be a grump at the same time?

Say:
- No!
- We can only do one or the other, like some other opposites.

Ask: *Allow time for answers.*
- Can you think of other opposites that you can't do at the same time? *Example: Being hungry and full at the same time.*
- If you are feeling grumpy, does praising God change what you are thinking about?
- Could this change your attitude?

Say:
- Let's give it a try.

Action:
- Divide the children into teams of one to three children.
- Give each team some paper and pencils or pens.
- Using the tune to the song that was chosen prior to the discussion, each team will change the words to create a new praise song.
- Allow time for them to work.
- Have each team sing the new praise song to everyone. *If they don't feel comfortable singing, they may read the words or everyone may sing the song together.*

Ask: *Allow time for answers.*
- Did your thoughts change while rewriting the song and praising God?

Final Thought:
Praising God helps us focus on Him and our blessings. Changing our thoughts helps change our attitudes. Most importantly, praise shows God our love and appreciation for Him and all that He does for us.

Christian Living

Chapter 5: Praise

Why Praise God? — Activities

Craft: Praise Decorations
Items Needed:
- General: Scissors and Markers or Crayons
- Per Child: 1 Sheet of Construction Paper or Card Stock Paper (precut into 4 squares)

Instructions:
- Give the children the supplies.
- Using the supplies, each child will decorate each sheet of paper with words and drawings that represent reasons to praise God.
- The sheets will be hung on the wall to fill the room with praises to God.

Indoor Activity: Alphabet Praise
Items Needed:
- 2 Bowls or Baskets and 2 Sets of Index Cards (cut into small pieces with the alphabet written on them)

Instructions:
- Place one set of the alphabet in each bowl or basket.
- Each bowl or basket will be placed in separate areas of the room on tables.
- Divide the children into two teams.
- Using their set of letters, each team will create words for blessings from God.
- Each team will use as many of the letters as they can.
- Give the teams 3 to 5 minutes to work.
- The team that uses the most letters wins the game.

Variation:
- The team with the most words is the winner.

Outdoor Activity: Bubble Praise
Prior to Activity:
- Mix ingredients together and stir.

Items Needed:
- General: Metal Coat Hanger (shaped into a bubble wand), Large Wide Bowl, 2 Cups Water, 1/2 Cup Dish Soap, and 1/4 Cup Corn Syrup

Instructions:
- Choose one child to be The Bubbler and start the game.
- The Bubbler will dip the bubble wand into the bubble solution.
- When the Bubbler creates a bubble, he or she will shout out a praise to God before anyone is able to pop the bubble.
- If another child pops the bubble before a praise is shouted out, he or she becomes the Bubbler.
- If a praise is called out before the bubble is popped, the Bubbler remains the same.

Safety:
- Only The Bubbler should have a wand during the game.

Fellowship and Praise

Prior to Discussion
- Have a Bible available and ask for volunteers to read.

Discussion
Say:
- All throughout the Bible, people took time to praise God.
- Praise can be personal, as with King Nebuchadnezzar.

Read: Daniel 4:37
Say:
- Another example of personal praise is when Jesus healed ten men of leprosy and only one of the men returned and praised God.

Read: Luke 17:15-16
Say:
- Praise can also be part of fellowship.

Ask: *Allow time for discussion.*
- Can you tell me what fellowship means?

Say:
- Fellowship is spending time with people who have interests similar to your own.

Ask: *Allow time for discussion.*
- Can you list some interests that you share with someone else?

Say:
- Fellowship and praise can begin after a great event.
- An example of this is when Moses and the Israelites broke out in praise after crossing the Red Sea.

Read: Exodus 14:29
Read: Exodus 15:1
Say:
- Another example of fellowship and praise is after the shepherds visited baby Jesus.

Read: Luke 2:20
Say:
- Fellowship and praise can also be a planned mission of praise with instruments and music.
- David planned a mission of praise while bringing the Ark of the Covenant into Jerusalem.

Read: 1 Chronicles 15:16
Say:
- Planning a time of fellowship and praise is extra special because it fulfills the requirements of Jesus' promise.

Read: Matthew 18:20
Say:
- Spending time with our Lord during a time of fellowship and praise makes the praise even more special!

Final Thought:
Praising God during our quiet time is important for our own spiritual growth. Praising God with fellowship among other believers is extra special, because Jesus promised to show up. Let's make time this week to combine some fellowship and praise.

Chapter 5: Praise

Fellowship and Praise — Activities

Craft: Musical Praise

Items Needed:
- General: Hole Punch and Markers
- Per Child: 2 Heavy Paper Plates, 4 Pipe Cleaners (cut in half), and 8 bells

Instructions:
- Give the children the supplies.
- The children will decorate the bottom of each plate.
- Placing the plates together with bottoms facing out, they will punch a hole through both plates along the edges.
- Matching the holes, they will use a pipe cleaner to fasten the plates and a bell together.
- They will punch another hole on the other side of the plates, match the holes and fasten the plates and bell together with a pipe cleaner.
- This will continue until they have punched eight holes in the plates and fastened the plates and bells with the pipe cleaners.
- Pipe cleaners may be twisted or twirled to use as a decoration.

Indoor Activity: Praising Him

Instructions:
- Have the children stand in a circle.
- Choose one child to say one thing for which he or she wants to praise God.
- The children will raise their hands and skip around in a circle singing, "Thank you God for {adding the child's answer}"
- As they sing, they will fill in the blank.
- When they return to where they started, the next child will give an answer.
- The children will raise their hands and skip around in a circle singing, "Thank you God for {adding the child's answer}."
- As they sing, they will repeat the first word of praise and the new one.
- They will continue until each child has been able to praise God for something.

Variation:
- Use different motions while moving around in a circle: hopping, twirling, walking backward or sideways, etc.

Outdoor Activity: Praise Circle

Items Needed:
- Per Child: Strips of Paper, Pencils or Pens, and a Bag or Box

Instructions:
- Give each child several strips of paper and pencils or pens.
- Ask the children to write down ways they can praise God.
- Have them put the ideas in the box or bag.
- Have the children stand in a circle.
- Choose one child to take an idea from the box or bag and read it out loud.
- All of the children will act out the idea while skipping or hopping around the circle.
- When the children return to their original spot, the child who retrieved the idea will choose another child to retrieve another idea from the box or bag for the children to act out.
- This will continue until all of the ideas have been acted out.

Praising God

Prior to Discussion
- Have a Bible available and ask for volunteers to read.

Discussion

Ask: *Allow time for discussion.*
- When we are moving around, singing, playing an instrument, or praising God in any other way, what should be our focus?

Say:
- God should be our focus if we are praising Him.

Ask: *Allow time for discussion.*
- If we are singing and clapping to a praise song and thinking about eating ice cream or a family trip, are we praising God?

Say:
- No, we are having fun and singing a praise song.

Ask: *Allow time for answers.*
- Do you think God likes it when we sing praise songs, even if we are thinking about ice cream or a family trip?

Say:
- Praise music is a great kind of music to sing and listen to!
- Truly praising God is when our thoughts are all about Him.
- In Old Testament times, the Levites worked in the temple.
- One of their jobs was to praise the Lord every morning and evening.

Read: 1 Chronicles 23:30
Say:
- True praise is proclaiming our love for the Father, Jesus, and the Holy Spirit.

Read: Ephesians 5:19-20
Say:
- Praise is focusing on how good God is to us.
- We are able to focus our thoughts on:
  » His grace: giving us what we don't deserve
  » His mercy: withholding what we do deserve
  » His blessings: everything we are and have

Ask: *Allow time for discussion.*
- What are some examples of God's grace, mercy, and blessings?

Say:
- Some examples are:
  » God's Love
  » The World
  » Salvation
  » Jesus
  » God's Guidance
  » the Holy Spirit
  » Pastors
  » Family (through birth and through Jesus)
  » Friends (especially faithful friends)

Read: Psalm 145
Read: Psalm 103

Final Thought:

Singing or speaking praises with our thoughts focused on God is a great way to proclaim our love and gratitude for God. We proclaim it to Him, the world, and our own selves. Our words say just how much we love God and the reasons for our love. This is truly praising our Lord.

Chapter 5: Praise

Praising God — Activities

Craft: Praising Him Frame

Items Needed:
- General: Craft Sticks, String or Yarn, Glue, Writing Pencil, and Markers or Colored Pencils
- Per Child: 1 Plastic Mirror, 1 Photo, OR 1/4 Sheet of Drawing Paper, 1 Sheet of Construction Paper (for variation)

Instructions:
- Give the children the supplies.
- If you are using the drawing paper, they will each draw their portrait on the paper.
- The sticks will be used to create a frame around the mirror, photo, or portrait.
- The string or yarn will be used to create a hanger.
- Using the pencil and pressing lightly, they will write, "PRAISING" on the top stick and, "HIM" on the bottom stick on the frame.
- They will then go over the pencil marking with a marker or colored pencil.
- While they are working, open a discussion: reasons to praise God.

Mission Project:
- This craft may be given to people in nursing homes and home bound family and friends.

Variation:
- To have praising hands on the frame, using construction paper, they will trace their hand, cut the hand shapes from the construction paper, and glue the hands on the top corners of the frame.

Indoor Activity: Remember to Praise

Instructions:
- Have the children sit in a circle.
- Choose one child to start the game.
- The first child will say, "I praise God for _____."
- When they say the sentence, they will fill in the blank.
- The child next to the first child will repeat what the first child said and add to it another praise.
- This will continue, with each child repeating everything that was already said and adding one new praise.
- If a child can't remember everything that was said, he or she is out of the game.
- The last child to praise God for everything that was mentioned wins the game.

Outdoor Activity: Praise God Relay

Instructions:
- This is a relay race.
- Divide the children into two teams.
- The children will begin at the starting line and race one at a time to the relay line.
- When a child gets to the relay line, he or she will shout out a praise to God.
- The child will then run back to the starting line and another child will to take his or her turn.
- They are to take turns until all of the players have shouted praise to God.
- The first team with all of their members back at the starting line wins the game.

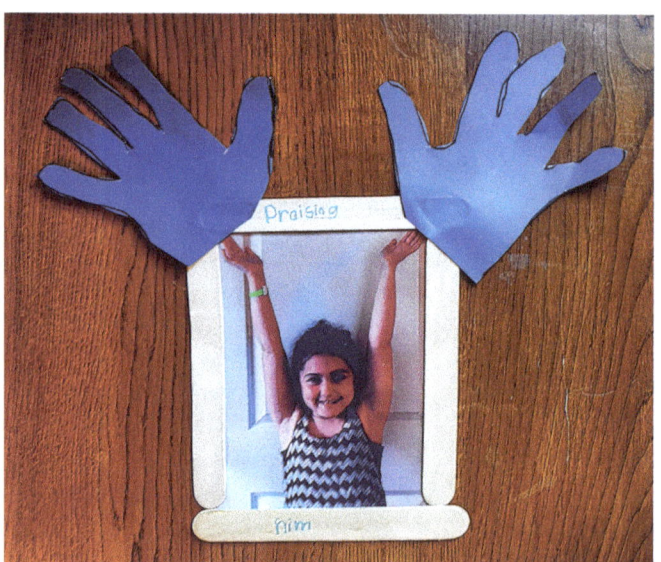

Addison with her Praising God Frame

Page 54 — Christian Living

Chapter 6
Forgiven

Hunting for FORGIVENESS

What is Forgiveness?

Discussion: "What is Forgiveness?" explains what forgiveness really is, that we, as God's people, are expected to do it too, and why.
Craft: Fishing For Forgiveness Game
Indoor Activity: Verse Mix Up
Outdoor Activity: Hunt for FORGIVENESS

Why is Forgiveness Important?

Discussion: "Why is Forgiveness Important" discusses anger and forgiveness, how they go together and what God thinks of both.
Craft: The Situation Book
Indoor Activity: oFISHally the Best
Outdoor Activity: Forgiven Tag

Forgiving Others

Discussion: "Forgiving Others" gives practical application for how to do that.
Craft: Finger Puppets
Indoor Activity: Forgiveness Theater
Outdoor Activity: Working Together Race

Forgiven

Discussion: "Forgiven" explains our own need for forgiveness and how our gracious God provided a way for that to happen.
Craft: Sharing Forgiveness
Indoor Activity: Forgiven Fruit
Outdoor Activity: Forgiven Relay

Christian Living

Chapter 6: Forgiven

Devotional Doodles

God's View

Draw a picture from God's view in Heaven.

The Challenge!

Can YOU find and memorize these verses?

Matthew 6:14-15

Matthew 5:23-24

Matthew 5:44

John 3:16

Romans 3:22-24

Romans 10:9-10

1 John 1:9

How Many

words can you make using these letters
FORGIVING FRUIT

_____   _____
_____   _____
_____   _____
_____   _____
_____   _____
_____   _____
_____   _____

Find the Words

```
F K H J E T U C F E
B O P R E E E R O F
L O R Y S S I R R K
O A I G U B U T G I
O I G L I I E S I N
D T H S R V J N V D
S R T B E L E O E N
T E R I S E I W N E
Z W A S L O V E X S
R W A S H E D G E S
```

FORGIVEN   LOVE   SNOW
FORGIVE   KINDNESS   JESUS
RIGHT   WASHED   BLOOD

Christian Living

What is Forgiveness?

Prior to Discussion
- Have a Bible available and ask for volunteers to read.

Discussion
Ask: *Allow time for discussion.*
- What is forgiveness?
- Is forgiveness an act of love?

Say:
- Listen to Jesus' words.

Read: Matthew 5:43-48

Say:
- Jesus tells us that we are to love and pray for those with whom we are angry, those who have wronged us.
- Love and prayer are actions, things that we intentionally do.
- This is especially true for those who have wronged us.
- When we love and pray for others, it becomes easier to overlook their shortcomings and failures and forgive them.

Ask: *Allow time for answers and discussion.*
- What does Jesus say about forgiving others?
- Do you believe that Jesus' words are reliable?

Say:
- Listen to His words about forgiveness.

Read: Matthew 6:14-15

Ask: *Allow time for answers.*
- Why do we need forgiveness from God?

Read: Romans 3:22-24

Say:
- Everyone has sinned and needs God's forgiveness!
- We don't deserve His forgiveness or to live with Him in Heaven.
- But . . . God loves us.
- God provided a way for us to be forgiven, because He loves us.

Read: John 3:16

Final Thought:

Jesus' love for us motivated Him to pay the price for our sins. Through Jesus, we are righteous, sinless, forgiven, and able to live with God in Heaven. He expects us to love and pray for others with that same forgiving love.

Chapter 6: Forgiven

What is Forgiveness?   Activities

Craft: Fishing for Forgiveness Game
Items Needed:
- General: Scissors and Markers and Pencils
- Per Child: 2 Sheets of Construction Paper (the same color), 8 Metal Paperclips, 1 Stick, 1 Craft Magnet, and 3 or 4 Feet of String

Instructions:
- Give each child the stick, magnet, and string.
- Each child will tie one end of the string to one end of the stick to make a fishing pole.
- The magnet will be tied to the other end of the string.
- They will cut each piece of construction paper into 4 equal pieces and fold each piece in half.
- Without cutting the folded side, have them cut out a fish shape out of each folded piece of construction paper and write their own name on each one.
- They will open four fish shapes and write words or draw pictures that represent forgiveness. *Examples: Forgiven, Love, and Prayer*
- In the other four fish shapes, they will write words or draw pictures that represent un-forgiveness. *Examples: Angry, Mad, and Hate*
- They will close the fish shapes and slide a paperclip onto the open side of each one so it stays closed.
- Tell them they can now play their game with their friends and family.

Game Instructions:
- Place the fish on the floor and give each player a certain amount of time to fish.
- The player who catches the most forgiveness fish wins the game.

Indoor Activity: Verse Mix Up
Prior to Activity:
- Create one set of verse cards for each team by writing one or two words from John 3:16 on each index card.

Items Needed:
- 2 Baskets, 2 Sets of Verse Cards, and 2 Bibles

Instructions:
- Divide the children into two teams and have them line up side by side.
- Place one set of verse cards in each basket.
- Give each team one basket and one Bible.
- The teams will work together to put the verse in the correct order.
- The first team with the verse in the correct order wins the game.

Additional Forgiveness Verses:
Matthew 5:22-23, Luke 6:37, Matthew 6:14-15, Ephesians 4:32

Outdoor Activity: Hunt for FORGIVENESS
Items Needed:
- Per Team: 1 Paper Lunch Bag

Instructions:
- Divide the children into teams of 2 or 3.
- Give each team a paper bag.
- Have each team find things outside that start with each letter of: FORGIVENESS.
- The team that gets all of their items first, wins the game.

Variation:
- The game can be timed, and the team with the most items wins the game.
- This game can be played again with different words: LOVE, HOLY SPIRIT, JESUS, etc.

Leah with her Fishing for Forgiveness Game

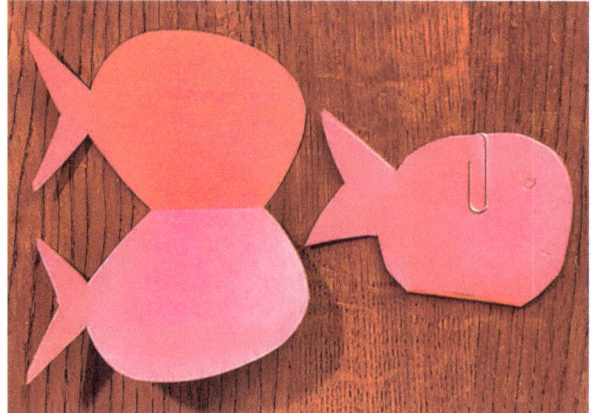

Chapter 6: Forgiven

Why is Forgiveness Important?

Prior to Discussion
- Have a Bible available and ask for volunteers to read.

Discussion
Ask: *Allow time for discussion.*
- Have you ever been angry with anyone?

Say:
- Listen to Jesus' words about anger as recorded by Matthew.

Read: Matthew 5:21-22a *(first sentence only)*
Ask: *Allow time for discussion.*
- What do you think Jesus is saying about anger?
- If we are angry with someone, are we sinning?

Say:
- At times, Jesus and God were angry.
- It is not a sin to be angry but it is a sin when we don't forgive others.
- Jesus goes on to tell us just how important it is to get rid of anger toward others.

Read: Matthew 5:23-24
Say:
- Jesus is talking about offerings, or things we give to God.

Ask: *Allow time for discussion.*
- What are some things we give God? *time, money, talents, loving others, sharing the Gospel, etc.*

Say:
- Jesus said if you want to offer God something and someone has something against you, go make it right first.
- Before God accepts our offerings, we must go make things right with the people in our lives.

Ask: *Allow time for answers.*
- Does it sound a bit like loving your enemies?

Read: Matthew 5:44
Say:
- He didn't say it's easy to love and pray for these people; He said we need to.

Ask: *Allow time for discussion.*
- Have you made someone angry?
- Has someone made you angry?
- Do you think there is a need for forgiveness when someone is angry?
- What is forgiveness?
- Why is it important for us to forgive others?

Say:
- Jesus answers this question for us.
- Listen carefully to Jesus' words on forgiveness.

Read: Matthew 6:14-15
Say:
- Let's pretend that you are angry with someone for doing wrong against you.
- Let's say you have not, and don't want to, forgive him or her.

Ask: *Allow time for discussion.*
- Should you forgive him or her if it was not your fault and they didn't ask for forgiveness?
- If not, when you mess up, will God forgive you?
- If not, will God accept an offering from you?
- Is forgiving others really important?

Final Thought:
God's forgiveness and His acceptance of our offerings are two great reasons to make sure we continuously forgive other people's wrongdoings. Forgiveness comes easier when we love and pray for them. Forgiving is something that we must actively do often, and it makes God very happy.

Christian Living

Chapter 6: Forgiven

Why is Forgiveness Important?   Activities

Craft: The Situation Book
Items Needed:
- General: Glue, Miscellaneous Decorations, and Crayons or Markers
- Per Child: Book Pages (3 sheets of white copy paper sewn down the middle and folded), and 1 Sheet of Construction Paper

Instructions:
- Give each child a set of book pages.
- Tell the children to fold the pages on the sewn line and wrap the construction paper around the book pages.
- Have them each glue the construction paper to the first page of the front and the last page of the back of the book pages to create a cover.
- They will each write, "The Situation" on the cover of their book and decorate it with the supplies.
- After they have decorated the books, call out a phrase and have the children write the phrase and a description of the details surrounding the phrase. *See sample phrases below.*
- The description can be words or pictures describing the context, location, and scene for the phrase.
- After all of the phrases have been used, have each child choose one phrase and description to share with everyone.

Sample Phrases:
- "That's very sticky!"
- "Forgive you for that?"
- "Time to get wet!"
- "God forgave me for this!"
- "Jump in!"
- "I'm truly forgiven!"

Indoor Activity: oFISHally the Best
Items Needed:
- General: Markers or Crayons, Scrap Construction Paper, Miscellaneous Decorations, Scissors, Glue, and Tape
- Per Grandparent Gift: Construction Paper and Small Pack of Fish Crackers

Instructions:
- Using the construction paper, each child will create a cover for a pack of crackers.
- On the cover they will each write "oFISHally the Best Grandparent Ever!"
- Using the supplies, they will each decorate their cover and tape it to the pack of crackers.
- Tell them that they may give these to their grandparents or someone who may be a stand-in grandparent.

Outdoor Activity: Forgiven Tag
Instructions:
- Divide the children into two teams. It is not necessary for the Teams to have an equal number of children.
- One team is the Forgiven Team and the other is the Un-Forgiven Team.
- The Forgiven Team's goal is to chase and tag all of the Un-Forgiven Team's members.
- As the Un-Forgiven Team members get tagged, they will become part of the Forgiven Team and help tag the Un-Forgiven Team's members.
- When all of the Un-Forgiven members have been tagged, the teams will switch roles; the Un-Forgiven Team is then the Forgiven Team and the Forgiven Team will then be the Un-Forgiven Team.

Addison with her Situation Book

Forgiving Others

Prior to Discussion
- Have a Bible available and ask for volunteers to read.
- Have available a white board, chalkboard, or poster board and something with which to write.

Discussion
Action:
- Write the children's answers to the following question on the board.

Ask: *Write down answers on board.*
- What are some relationships that you have with other people? *Examples: parent/child, cousins, friends, and classmates.*

Ask: *Allow time for discussion.*
- In any of these relationships, have you ever had an argument or a disagreement?
- If so, how long did the argument last?
- Should you wait to forgive so you can be mad for a while?
- Do you think a week, month, or year would be too long to wait before forgiveness is given?
- Should we forgive someone even if he or she never asks for forgiveness?
- Does it seem impossible to forgive some people?
- Does God expect us to forgive everyone for everything?

Say:
- Listen to Jesus' words.

Read: Matthew 6:14-15

Ask: *Allow time for answers.*
- What does this mean?

Say:
- When we forgive others, Jesus promises us that God will forgive us.
- Jesus says that we are to do more than just forgive them.
- He says we are to love and pray for them.

Read: Matthew 5:44

Ask: *Allow time for answers.*
- Do you WANT to be loving to someone who is not kind to you?
- Can it be tough to pray for God to bless him or her?
- Think of someone who has done something to you and your response was to become angry.

Action:
- Make sure each child has someone in mind.

Ask: *Allow time for discussion.*
- Do you, **right now**, WANT to pray that God will bless him or her in a very special way?
- How about in such a special way that he or she knows the blessing could have only come from God?
- Do you think most people would feel the same way you do? Why?

Say:
- Let's take some time right now for any of you who want to pray for anyone with whom you may be angry.

Action:
- Allow time for the children to pray.
- The leader may lead the prayer or allow the children to pray individually.

Final Thought:
Jesus said we should love and pray for our enemies. These are people who have done wrong to us for some reason. Forgiveness comes as we love and pray for them. It is looking at him or her and asking God to bless them instead of desiring revenge. True forgiveness produces the fruit of the Spirit in our relationship with those who have done wrong toward us. Let's remember to love and pray for people, instead of focusing on the anger and hatred.

Chapter 6: Forgiven

Forgiving Others — Activities

Craft: Finger Puppets

Items Needed:
- General: Ruler, Scissors, Felt Scraps, Craft Glue, Googly Eyes, Markers, Fabric Scraps, and Miscellaneous Decorations

Instructions:
- Each child will cut two 2" x 3" pieces of felt.
- The felt will be glued together along the top and side edges; leaving the bottom edge open.
- Each set of rectangle shapes will become one puppet.
- After the glue dries, the children will trim the corners from the top of the rectangle and it will become the puppet's head.
- Using the supplies, the children will decorate the puppets to create different characters.

Indoor Activity: Forgiveness Theater

Items Needed:
- Picnic Items: Puppets, Popcorn, and Drinks

Instructions:
- Set up the room like a theater with chairs in rows facing a table that is the stage.
- Give the children popcorn and drinks to snack on while they watch the show.
- The children will take turns as teams or individually and use the puppets to tell a story of forgiveness.
- The story may be from the Bible or from their own lives.

Outdoor Activity: Working Together Race

Items Needed:
- 2 Balls (balls that are soft)

Instructions:
- This is a race, so there needs to be a starting point and an ending point.
- Divide the children into two teams and give each team a ball.
- Each team will line up at the starting point.
- The first two children in each team will move as fast as they can while tossing the ball back and forth until they get to the finish line.
- One of the children will run back with the ball and the next person in line will join him or her in tossing the ball back and forth until they get to the finish line.
- The "new" child will then run back with the ball and the next child in line will join in and toss the ball back and forth until they reach the finish line.
- The team whose members reach the finish line first, wins the game.
- If there is an uneven number of children, one of the first children to toss the ball will go to the end of the line and play again on the team that is short one person.

Variation:
- If the ball is dropped, the two team members must return to the starting line and begin again.

Forgiven

Prior to Discussion
- Have a Bible available and ask for volunteers to read.

Discussion
Ask: *Allow time for discussion.*
- What does it mean to be forgiven?
- What do we have to do for God to forgive us?

Read: Matthew 6:14-15
Ask: *Allow time for answers.*
- The Bible tells us that we must also confess our sins to be forgiven.

Read: 1 John 1:9
Ask: *Allow time for discussion.*
- What does it mean to be forgiven by God?
- Why do we need God's forgiveness?

Read: Romans 4:7-8
Say:
- So, if our sins are forgiven, we will be blessed.
- We know that we have to confess our sins.

Ask: *Allow time for answers.*
- What next?

Say:
- God loves us so much that He sent His only Son to take the punishment for our sins.

Read: John 3:16
Say:
- God's love is so great that He provided a way for us to be forgiven and cleansed of our sins.
- God has blessed each of us with the ability to accept His Son and confess our sins, which will be covered by Jesus' blood.
- Our sins will no longer be counted against us.
- This is true forgiveness.
- When we put our trust in Jesus and accept His gift, we become righteous and gain eternal life.

Read: 2 Corinthians 5:21
Ask: *Allow time for answers.*
- What does all of this mean?
- What does God's forgiveness and our becoming righteous mean?

Say:
- Because of Jesus, God totally and completely forgives us, even though we haven't done anything to deserve it.
- We only need to accept what Jesus did as God's one and only Son.
- Listen to this verse as Paul explains what it all means to us.

Read: Romans 10:9-10
Final Thought:
Loving and praying for others are two ways to show Jesus that we love Him. These actions produce forgiveness in our relationships with those who have done wrong toward us. True love is what God feels for us and is the reason for His gift of forgiveness. Forgiveness from God comes when we forgive others and confess our sins. When we repent and Jesus becomes our Savior, we are righteous and promised eternal life follow.

Forgiven — Activities

Craft: Sharing Forgiveness
Items Needed:
- General: Paint Brushes, Paint, Cups of Water (to rinse brushes), Miscellaneous Decorations, and Glue
- Per Child: 1 Rock or Shell and 1 Apron

Instructions:
- Each child will put on an apron to protect his or her clothing.
- Using the supplies, the children will decorate the rocks or shells to represent Jesus' gift of forgiveness.
- They will each give their rock or shell to someone and share how to be forgiven of our sins.

Indoor Activity: Forgiven Fruit
Items Needed:
- Per Child - 1 Bible, 1 Sheet of Paper, and 1 Pencil

Instructions:
- Each player will write **FORGIVEN** vertically (top to bottom) on the paper.
- Using the Bible, each player will find Galatians 5:22-23, which lists the fruits, of the Spirit.
- Each player will use the fruit-words to create an acrostic using each letter in the word **FORGIVEN**.
- The letter does not have to be the first letter of the fruit. For example the **O** in one of the fruit may be used instead of the **L** in love, **J** in joy, or **G** in goodness.
- See solution in Supplemental Material section on page 86.

Outdoor Activity: Forgiven Relay
Items Needed:
- White Cotton Balls, Glue, 2 White Poster Boards, Markers

Instructions:
- Divide the children into two teams and give each team a poster board and markers.
- Have each team write sins and good deeds on their poster board, making sure there are an equal amount on each poster board.
- Tell them this is a relay race and they will be using the cotton to cover the sins.
- From the starting line, one member from each team will run to the relay line with one piece of cotton.
- They will use the glue to glue their pieces of cotton over one of the sins and will then run back to the starting line.
- The next child will take one piece of cotton and use the glue to cover another sin.
- This will continue until all of the sins are covered.
- The first team to cover all of the sins wins the game.

Variation:
- Teams must swap boards before the race.

Chapter 7
Spiritual Gifts

TJ with his Planting Gift

What are Spiritual Gifts?
Discussion: "What are Spiritual Gifts" discusses where they are from and why we have them.
Craft: Spiritual Gifts Poster
Indoor Activity: Find the Gifts
Outdoor Activity: Planting Gifts

The Gifts
Discussion: "The Gifts" discusses different gifts and how they are used.
Craft: My Gift
Indoor Activity: Gifted Toes
Outdoor Activity: Working Together Race

I Have Gifts!
Discussion: "I Have Gifts!" encourages appreciation for our own special gifts, because each gift is a tool to meet a need.
Craft: Gifted Puppets
Indoor Activity: Gifts Analysis
Outdoor Activity: Gift Wrapping Relay

Using My Gifts
Discussion: "Using My Gifts" helps children understand that they and their gifts are part of the whole body of Christ and that all work together for the good of all.
Craft: The Body Chain
Indoor Activity: Statues
Outdoor Activity: The Body

Gifts and Love
Discussion: "Gifts and Love" explains how important love is when using our gifts or doing anything for our Lord.
Craft: Love Clips and Cards
Indoor Activity: Gift Skits
Outdoor Activity: Getting Ready Relay

Chapter 7: Spiritual Gifts

Devotional Doodles

God's View
Draw a picture of a gift.

The Challenge!
Can YOU find and memorize these verses?

1 Corinthians 12:1-3

1 Corinthians 13:13

Romans 12:6

1 Peter 4:10

Ephesians 4:11

Colossians 3:23-24

Matthew 22:37-39

10 Gifts
List Ten Spiritual Gifts
Romans 12:4-8 & Ephesians 4:11-13

1. _____
2. _____
3. _____
4. _____
5. _____
6. _____
7. _____
8. _____
9. _____
10. _____

Find the Words

I	K	H	G	R	A	C	E	S	E
G	L	P	L	A	O	E	R	P	F
H	O	L	Y	S	P	I	R	I	T
O	V	T	H	E	B	N	T	R	H
F	E	E	H	R	I	E	H	I	W
A	T	S	S	E	R	V	E	T	A
I	E	R	V	E	R	A	E	U	E
T	E	R	I	S	E	S	A	A	T
H	G	I	F	T	S	T	I	L	E
R	S	I	G	N	O	R	A	N	T

LOVE   HOLY SPIRIT   FAITH
GIFTS   SERVE   IGNORANT
SPIRITUAL   GRACE   OTHERS

Christian Living

What are Spiritual Gifts?

Prior to Discussion
- Have a Bible available and ask for volunteers to read.

Discussion
Ask: *Allow time for answers.*
- What are spiritual gifts?

Say:
- Spiritual gifts are like seeds planted before we are born that grow when God knows that it is time.
- Just like seeds planted in the soil, they grow at just the right time, when the weather, water, nutrients, and light is just right.
- That tiny plant that is so full of potential breaks out of the seed and becomes what God created it to be.
- God created us with special gifts to help us become all that He created us to be.
- God told Jeremiah that He knew him before he was even born.

Read: Jeremiah 1:5

Ask: *Allow time for answers.*
- Do you think He knew us before we were born as well?
- Do you think He has a job appointed to us like He did Jeremiah?

Say:
- God has a special job for each of us and our spiritual gifts help us with our job.
- Paul knew that it is important for people to understand their gifts.

Read: 1 Corinthians 12:1

Say:
- Ignorant means not knowing.
- Paul is telling us that it is important to know about the gifts that God has given you.

Ask: *Allow time for discussion.*
- When you discover your spiritual gifts, what should you do with them?

Say:
- Paul answered this question for us in his letter to the Colossian church.

Read: Colossians 3:23-24

Say:
- Paul said whatever we do, work for the Lord.
- There is something very important that we need to know when using our gifts.

Ask: *Allow time for discussion.*
- Can you tell me what this important thing is?

Say:
- Listen to what Paul said about this important part of using our gifts.

Read: 1 Corinthians 13:1-2

Say:
- Love is the most important part of using our gifts.

Final Thought:
God has given each of us spiritual gifts. He wants us to know all about them, use them for Him, and to help others. The key to using them is to always use them with love. Love is one key to pleasing God. Love Him first and most, and love others. As we use our gifts, let's remember to do it with love.

What are Spiritual Gifts? — Activities

Chapter 7: Spiritual Gifts

Craft: Spiritual Gifts Posters
Items Needed:
- General: Poster Boards, Tape, Crayons or Markers, Miscellaneous Decorations, Old Magazines, Glue, Construction Paper, Pencils, Erasers, and Scissors
- Per Child: 1 Sheet of White Paper and 1 Poster Board

Instructions:
- Give each child the supplies.
- They will each use the supplies to decorate their posters in a way that explains spiritual gifts.
- Tell them to use the white paper to draw what they want, make changes, and get it as close to perfect as they can.
- When they each know how they are going to decorate their poster, they will use their white paper drawings as a guide to put their creations on the poster boards.
- Each child should write the title, "Spiritual Gifts," on his or her poster.
- When they have finished their posters, each child will tell everyone about his or her poster.
- Each child will find a special spot on the wall to decorate the room with his or her poster.

Indoor Activity: Find the Gifts
Prior to Activity:
- Hide gifts around the room.

Items Needed:
- General: Small Gifts (Candy, Small Toys, Trinkets, etc.) and Crayons or Markers (optional)
- Per Child: 1 Bag

Instructions:
- Let the children know there are treasures hidden and they are to find them.
- Each time one is found, they have to celebrate like the angels in Heaven by saying, "Praise the Lord."
- The children may decorate the bags if there is time.

Outdoor Activity: Planting Gifts
Items Needed:
- General: Newspapers and Potting Soil
- Per Child: 1 Plant Pot, 1 Coffee Filter, and Several Flower or Vegetable Seeds (allow each child to choose which he or she would like to grow)

Instructions:
- Spread newspaper to protect the table that the children will be using for this activity.
- Give each child a plant pot.
- Have the children line the plant pot with the coffee filter to keep the soil in the pot.
- Tell the children to fill their pots three fifths the way with potting soil.
- Have them poke a hole in the soil to put the seeds in. (The hole should be approximately four times larger than the size of the seeds, but read the package directions for specific instructions.)
- Give each child some seeds and have them put their seeds in the hole in the soil.
- Tell them that the seeds will need to be watered and have some light so they will grow.
- If this is done away from home, it may be best to tell the children to water the plant when they get home so there is less mess on their trip home.
- While they are working, open a discussion about the gifts that are within seeds: acorns, cattails, cotton, flowers, fruit, and vegetables.

Variation:
- The children can do the activity as a group and take care of the plant together.

The Gifts

Prior to Discussion
- Have a Bible available and ask for volunteers to read.

Discussion
Ask: *Allow time for discussion.*
- What are spiritual gifts?

Say:
- Spiritual gifts are special abilities that we receive from God.
- They help us do all of the things that God created us to do.

Ask: *Allow time for answers.*
- Can you name some of the gifts of the Spirit?

Say:
- Paul explains some of the gifts of the Spirit in his letters.

Read: Romans 12:6-8
Read: Ephesians 4:11
Say:
- Let's talk about some of the spiritual gifts and people in the Bible who had each gift.
- Administration is being able to organize, make plans, and get the right people involved to get something done.
- God gave Nehemiah this gift so he could organize, plan, and motivate people to rebuild the walls in Jerusalem.
- Creative ability is the gift of creativity: arts, writing, drama, and music.
- King David and King Solomon used this gift to write songs and play musical instruments.
- Encouragement is the gift of comforting and encouraging others.
- Paul used this gift and his creative ability to write letters to individuals and churches.
- Because Paul used his gifts, we are still encouraged by his letters today.
- Evangelism is the gift of sharing the gospel.
- Philip used this gift when he talked to the Ethiopian about Jesus.
- A prophet receives messages from God to share with others.
- The last seventeen books of the Old Testament, Isaiah through Malachi, are books of prophets.
- There are many other gifts mentioned in the Bible:
  » a Giver loves to give,
  » a Preacher leads people into a relationship with Jesus,
  » a Prophet receives messages from God to share with others,
  » a Teacher explains things in a way that people can understand,
  » a Server loves to serve others.

Ask: *Allow time for answers.*
- Do you think spiritual gifts are important when we do things for God?

Say:
- God has given you the gifts that you need to fulfill your purpose.
- Just like the people in the Bible who had just the right gifts to get their missions done, you have just the right gift or gifts to get your mission done.

Final Thought:
An important thing to know about these spiritual gifts is that you have one or more of them. We all have a special mission and God gives us spiritual gifts to achieve our mission. Paying attention to the things that interest you and the things that you are good at is a great start to discovering your gifts. Once you know what they are, you can begin developing them, using them for God, and fulfilling His purpose for your life.

Chapter 7: Spiritual Gifts

The Gifts / Activities

Craft: My Gift
Items Needed:
- Per Child: A Portion of Play Dough

Instructions:
- Give each child a portion of play dough.
- They will each create something that represents a spiritual gift.
- Each child will explain the play dough creation to everyone.

Indoor Activity: Gifted Toes
Items Needed:
- General: 1 Bag of Wrapped Candy
- Per Child: 1 Paper Lunch Bag

Instructions:
- Spread the candy over the floor and give each child a bag.
- The children will pick up and place the candy in their bag, using only their toes.
- They may hold their bags with their hands.
- The child with the most candy in his or her bag wins the game.

Outdoor Activity: Working Together Race
Items Needed:
- 2 Pieces of Ribbon or Rope (long enough for 1/2 of the children to hold onto)

Instructions:
- Divide the children into two teams.
- Give each team a piece of ribbon or rope.
- Explain that each team member must hold onto the rope or ribbon while racing to the finish line and back.
- Tell them they will need to work together and pay attention to their team members, since some will not be able to run as fast as other members.
- The first team to return to the starting line wins the game.

Variation:
- Have the children run an obstacle course instead of running to a finish line and back.

I Have Gifts!

Prior to Discussion
- Have a Bible available and ask for volunteers to read.
- Have available: a mixing bowl, a whisk, 1/2 cup water, 1/8 cup of flour, a board, 1 - 1 to 2 inch nail, and a hammer with a claw.

Discussion
Ask: *Allow time for answers.*
- Do you think God has a special purpose for you?

Say:
- God created each of us with our own personality, spiritual gifts, and a special purpose.
- Paul said that we need to know about our spiritual gifts.

Read: 1 Corinthians 12:1
Say:
- Ignorant means not knowing.
- I am going to demonstrate just how important it is to know what your gifts are.

Action:
- Show the children the hammer and whisk.

Say:
- This is Happy Hammer and Wonder Whisk.
- Happy and Wonder are friends.
- Happy is great at hammering nails into boards.

Action:
- Use the hammer to hammer the nail into the board, but not all the way.

Say:
- Wonder wants to try hammering also.

Action:
- Use the whisk to hammer the nail into the board.

Say:
- Wonder is sad because he can't do what his friend is able to do.
- Sometimes God gives His children more than one gift.
- Happy is not only good at hammering nails into boards, but he is also good at something else.

Ask: *Allow time for answers.*
- What else can Happy Hammer do with a nail?

Say:
- Happy can pull nails out of boards.
- Wonder Whisk wants to try, because he might be able to do THIS.
- So, Happy Hammer lets Wonder Whisk try.

Action:
- Try pulling the nail out of the board with the whisk.

Say:
- Wonder can't do it!
- He feels really bad and says, "I can't do anything!"

Say:
- Wonder's owner needs to mix some ingredients together.

Action:
- Place water and flour into a bowl.

Say:
- Happy knows that Wonder is the man for this job!
- But Wonder doesn't even want to try because he failed two times already.
- Happy encourages him to try.
- He explains that hammers aren't good at mixing ingredients together.
- Wonder reluctantly agrees to try.

Ask: *Allow time for answers.*
- What do you think will happen?

Action:
- Mix the flour and water with the whisk.

Say:
- He did a great job and is very happy.

Final Thought:
We are not good at something just because we want to be or because our friends or family are good at something. God created each of us because He has a plan for our life. He gave each of us special gifts. When we find out what they are and how God wants us to use them, we will be great at what we do for God!

Chapter 7: Spiritual Gifts

I Have Gifts!   Activities

Craft: Gifted Puppets
Items Needed:
- General: Scissors, Crayons or Markers, Glue, and Scrap Construction Paper
- Per Child: 2 Craft Sticks and 1 Index Card

Instructions:
- Tell the children that they are going to create two stick puppets to play with and will pretend to give them spiritual gifts.
- Give each child two craft sticks and one index card.
- Tell the children to cut their index cards in half, cutting the longest sides.
- Have them each cut an oval out of each half of the index card. (These will be the faces of the puppets.)
- Have them decorate the faces.
- The remainder of the index card can be used for ears and hair.
- After they decorate the faces, they will glue the faces onto the sticks.
- They will use the supplies to decorate the sticks and will assign each puppet at least one gift.

Indoor Activity: Gift Analysis

Items Needed:
- Per Child: 1 Gifts Analysis Test for Children (The one I find helpful is *Discover God's Special Gifts for you Your Gifts for Children* by Dr. Larry Gilbert. Scan QR code or go to www.churchgrowth.org.

Instructions:
- These instructions are for the suggested book.
- Give each child a booklet and have the children take turns reading pages 3 to 13.
- Turn to page 14 and read the steps at the top of the page.
- Give the children time to complete the analysis.
- Each child will tell everyone his or her top two or three gifts and how they feel about each one.

Outdoor Activity: Gift Wrapping Relay
Items Needed:
- 2 Boxes (same size), Wrapping Paper or Newspaper (enough to cover boxes), and 2 Rolls of Tape

Instructions:
- Divide the children into two teams.
- Place one box at the relay line for each team and give each team one roll of tape.
- Each team will line up at the team's starting line.
- One at a time, each child will tear off a piece of tape, run to the relay line, and begin wrapping the box.
- When the tape has been used, the child will run back to the starting line.
- When the child crosses the starting line, the next child will tear off the tape, run to the relay line, and wrap more of the box.
- The children will continue taking turns until the box has been completely covered.
- The first team to have its box completely covered and have all members back at the starting line wins the game.

Variation:
- Each team member will have one turn instead of playing until the box is completely covered.

Using My Gifts

Prior to Discussion
- Have a Bible available and ask for volunteers to read.

Discussion
Ask: *Allow time for answers.*
- Do you ever feel like you don't need the help of others?
- Have you just wanted to do something all by yourself, without ANY help?

Say:
- God has given each of His children spiritual gifts.
- When Christians work together in love, each using his or her own spiritual gift, we are able to accomplish God's plans for His kingdom.
- Listen as Paul explains using spiritual gifts by comparing it to a body.

Read: 1 Corinthians 12:14-18, 26, 27
Ask: *Allow time for answers.*
- What do you think this means?

Say:
- Just as our body needs each part to be our best, Christians need each other and each other's gifts for the church, the body of Christ, to be at its best.

Ask: *Allow time for answers.*
- What do you think our focus should be while using our gifts?

Say:
- Listen to what Peter wrote about using our gifts.

Read: 1 Peter 4:8-11
Say:
- There are several things to remember from these verses.
- Peter said to love each other deeply, don't grumble, and serve others when using our gifts.
- The purpose of all of our gifts is that God may be praised.
- When we use our gifts, we can ask ourselves who benefits from what we are doing.

Final Thought:
Spiritual gifts are an important part of the life of a Christian. Each of us has our own special purpose that is part of God's plan, so He joins people together, each with his or her own special gifts. God wants us to work together to accomplish our special part of His plan. The ultimate goal is that God receives the praise and glory in all that we do.

Chapter 7: Spiritual Gifts

Using My Gifts — Activities

Craft: The Body Chain

Items Needed:
- General: Scissors, and Crayons or Markers
- Per Child: 1 Sheet of Construction Paper

Instructions:
- Give each child the paper.
- Have them fold the paper in half.
- Have them fold each edge over to the center fold, like an accordion.
- Tell them to cut out boys and girls, leaving the hands uncut so they will stay attached.
- While the children are working, open a discussion on ways we can work together with different gifts.
- They may assign each body a gift and decorate them.

Indoor Activity: Statues

Instructions:
- Explain that we can stand around like statues, or we can work toward completing God's purpose for our lives.
- The children will stand in a circle.
- The leader will call out, "Your job is to . . ." and fill in different actions.
- Examples: jump like a rabbit, turn in a circle, pat your head, jump on one foot, march, or say, "I love Jesus."
- The children will perform the action until the leader calls out, "Your job is to freeze!"
- All of the children will freeze and stand like a statue.
- The leader will call out different actions and freeze intermittently.
- If a child moves when he or she should be frozen, that child is out of the game.
- The last child to follow the commands completely wins the game.

Outdoor Activity: The Body

Instructions:
- This is a tag game.
- Choose two children to start the game.
- They will be the "body."
- They will lock their arms together without coming apart.
- When the "body" tags someone, that child will become part of the "body."
- They will lock arms with the other "body" children.
- The "body" will grow larger and larger.
- Only the children on the ends of the "body" will tag the other children.
- When all of the children have joined the "body," choose two children to start the game over again.

Christian Living

Gifts and Love

Prior to Discussion
- Have a Bible available and ask for volunteers to read.
- Have available: a whiteboard, chalkboard, or poster board and something with which you can write.
- Write on the board, "Love is: patient, kind, and rejoices in the truth." Below this write, "Love is NOT: envious, boastful, conceited, acting improperly, selfish, provoked, keeping a record of wrongs, and finding joy in unrighteousness."

Discussion
Ask: *Allow time for discussion.*
- What are spiritual gifts?

Say:
- They are special gifts that we receive from God to help us achieve our God-given purpose.
- Listen closely as I read from First Corinthians.
- See if you can tell me what we all need to have when using our spiritual gifts.

Read: 1 Corinthians 13:1-3

Ask: *Allow time for answers.*
- What is Paul's point here?
- What does love have to do with our spiritual gifts? *Reread verses if necessary.*

Say:
- Love is important when using our gifts because they are much more effective with love.
- So, it seems that love is pretty important to God!
- Jesus did give us the two greatest commandments and they both tell us to love.

Ask: *Allow time for answers.*
- What are Jesus' two greatest commands?

Read: Matthew 22:37-39

Say:
- Love is important to God!
- Our two greatest commands from Jesus are to love God first and most and love others the way we love ourselves.

Ask: *Allow time for answers.*
- What is love?

Say:
- Paul answers this for us in his first letter to the Corinthian church.

Action:
- Point to each word on the board as the verse is read.

Read: 1 Corinthians 13:4-6

Ask: *Allow time for answers.*
- If your teacher is NOT loving, would you enjoy learning?
- If your teacher is patient and kind, would he or she be a better teacher?

Say:
- Anytime we use our gifts with love, our work becomes better and more effective.

Final Thought:
God's Word tells us that love is important for our spiritual gifts to be effective. Love is so important to God that it is part of both of the two greatest commands that Jesus gave us. We need to remember to love, have patience, be kind, and rejoice in truth. God will be even more pleased and our work will be better and more effective.

Chapter 7: Spiritual Gifts

Gifts and Love — Activities

Craft: Love Clips and Cards
Items Needed:
- General: Pencils, Scissors, Crayons or Markers, and Glue
- Per Child: 1/2 Sheet of Construction Paper, 1 Craft Magnet, 1 Clothespin and 1 4x4-Inch Piece of Cardboard (empty cereal boxes work well for this)

Instructions:
- Tell the children that they will make a clip and a card to hang in the clip.
- The clips and cards will be given to the people they love.
- The children will each fold the construction paper in half and create a card.
- They will each draw a picture on the cardboard, color the picture, and cut it out.
- They will each glue their picture to one side of the clothespin with the part that you grasp on top.
- They will each glue the magnet to the other side of the clothespin so it can be hung to display the card or artwork.
- These may be given to someone who is using a spiritual gift with love or to evangelize to someone who needs to know about Jesus' love.
- While they work, open a discussion about people around us who use their gifts with love. *Pastors, teachers, singers, servers, counselors, etc.*

Indoor Activity: Gift Skits
Items Needed:
- General: Paper Bag and Pencils or Pens
- Per Child: 2 Pieces of Scrap Paper and 1 Bible

Instructions:
- Have each child write one gift of the spiritual gifts on each piece of paper. (See 1 Corinthians 12:7-10)
- Divide the children into teams of two or three children.
- Each child will draw one piece of paper from the bag.
- The teams will work together to make up a skit with each person in the skit using the gift that was drawn from the bag.
- Teams will take turns performing their skits for everyone.

Variation:
- This can be done individually instead of as teams.

Outdoor Activity: Getting Ready Relay
Items Needed:
- 2 Suitcases or Overnight Bags, 2 Sets of Traveling Supplies (toothbrushes, toothpaste, brush or comb, soap, pajama top, extra shirt, etc.)

Instructions:
- Explain that we should be as ready as possible when God calls us to do a job for Him.
- This is a relay race.
- Divide the children into two teams and give each team one set of the traveling supplies.
- Each team will pretend to help pack the supplies needed for a trip on which a gifted evangelist is going to spread the gospel.
- One at a time, each child will race to the relay line, taking one item, placing it in the suitcase or overnight bag, and running back to the starting line.
- When the child crosses the starting line, the next child will take his or her turn.
- The first team to pack all of the items for the evangelist and have all members back at the starting line wins the game.

Additional Information

Coming SOON!!!
- Life and Times of Jesus (35 discussions)
- The Transition to Kings (22 discussions)
- Creation Explorers in the Garden
- Creation Explorers in Nature
- The Bible Collection:
    ◊ The Bible (4 discussions)
    ◊ The Testaments (4 discussions)
    ◊ Old Testament The Law (26 discussions)
    ◊ Old Testament History (57 discussions)

Visit: www.christianconceptsforkids.com to find out more!

Supplemental Material

Spiritual Armor Craft (long-term project located on page 41):
- Craft Sample   Page 78
- Soldier Cutout   Page 79
- Armor Cutouts   Page 80

Forgiven Fruit Indoor Activity (located on page 69):
- Forgiven Fruit Solution   Page 81

About Karen Palmer

Karen Palmer is married with 4 adult children and 9 grandchildren. She, her husband, and three dogs currently live in South Carolina where she loves spending time with family and friends, gardening, writing, going on nature walks, and being outdoors.

Karen's years of service in various children's ministries, gift of teaching, passion for sharing Christ, and love for children has led her to write lessons that are scripted discussions of Christian concepts that are written with the elementary-aged child in mind.

Her goal is for each child to grow in his or her relationship with Christ, clearly understand each concept, apply it in his or her own life, and share it with friends and family.

Karen's years as a Master Gardener and a Master Naturalist, leading nature walks, gardening, and love for nature have given her experience and insight into sharing God's amazing world, flora, and fauna with others in her Creation Explorers books and some of the activities in this Christian Living book.

Writing books that are engaging and help children interact and discuss the amazing world God created and important concepts that help us live a great Christian life are something that adds to Karen's excitement in life. She believes it is a blessing to be able to share what she knows and loves.

What is Spiritual Armor?

Additional Information

Sample Craft

Additional Information

What is Spiritual Armor? | Soldier Cutout

Christian Living

Additional Information

What is Spiritual Armor?

Armor Cutout

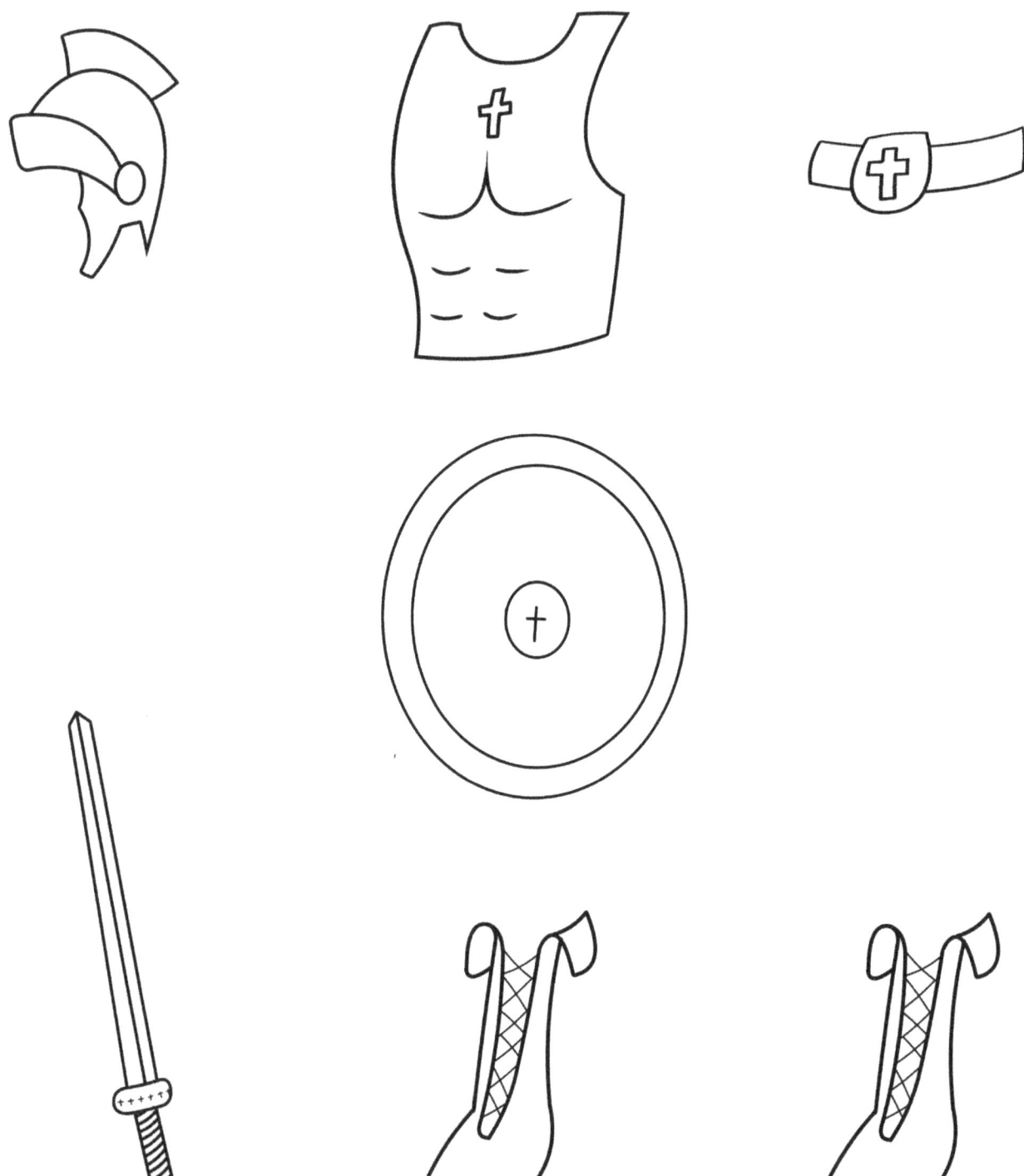

Christian Living

Additional Information

Forgiven

Forgiven Fruit Solution

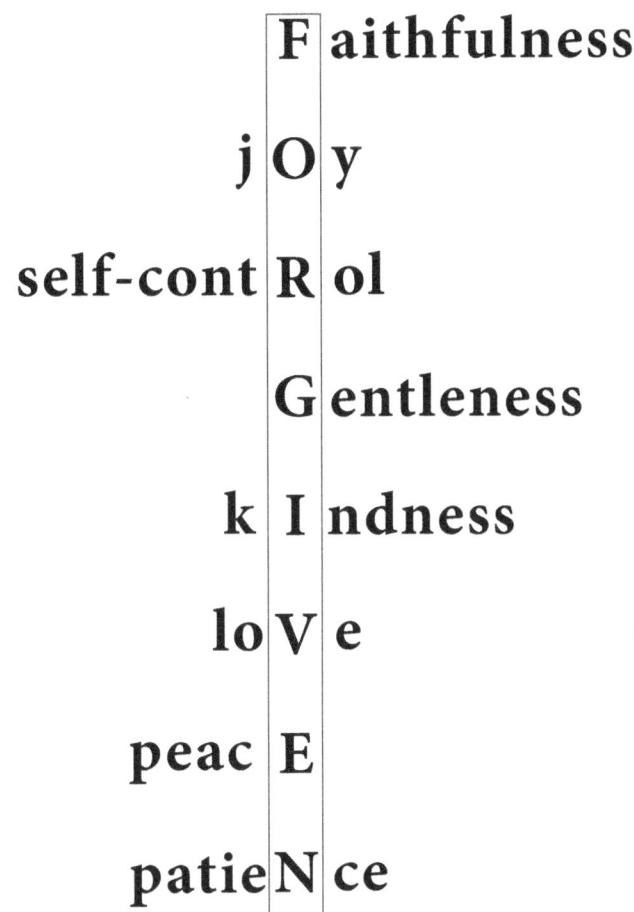

                    F aithfulness
                     j O y
          self-cont R ol
                   G entleness
                k I ndness
               lo V e
             peac E
           patie N ce

Fruit of the Spirit

Love	Patience	Faithfulness
Joy	Kindness	Gentleness
Peace	Goodness	Self-Control

Christian Living